THE CHURCH AT WORSHIP: CASE STUDIES FROM CHI

MW00576528

Series Editors: LESTER RUTH, CARRIE STEENWYK, JOHN D. WITVLIET

Published

Walking Where Jesus Walked: Worship in Fourth-Century Jerusalem
    Lester Ruth, Carrie Steenwyk, John D. Witvliet

Tasting Heaven on Earth: Worship in Sixth-Century Constantinople
    Walter D. Ray

*Longing for Jesus: Worship at a Black Holiness Church
in Mississippi, 1895–1913*
    Lester Ruth

*Lifting Hearts to the Lord: Worship with John Calvin
in Sixteenth-Century Geneva*
    Karin Maag

*Worshiping with the Anaheim Vineyard: The Emergence
of Contemporary Worship*
    Andy Park, Lester Ruth, and Cindy Rethmeier

*Leaning on the Word: Worship with Argentine Baptists
in the Mid-Twentieth Century*
    Lester Ruth and Eric L. Mathis

Leaning

on the Word

Worship with Argentine Baptists in the Mid-Twentieth Century

LESTER RUTH AND ERIC L. MATHIS

William B. Eerdmans Publishing Company
Grand Rapids, Michigan

WM. B. EERDMANS PUBLISHING CO.
2140 Oak Industrial Drive N.E., Grand Rapids, Michigan 49505
www.eerdmans.com

26 25 24 23 22 21 20 19 18 17   1 2 3 4 5 6 7 8 9 10

ISBN 978-0-8028-7390-3

Library of Congress Cataloging-in-Publication Data

Names: Ruth, Lester, 1959– author. | Mathis, Eric L.
Title: Leaning on the word : worship with Argentine Baptists in the mid-twentieth century /
    Lester Ruth and Eric L. Mathis.
Description: Grand Rapids, Michigan : William B. Eerdmans Publishing Company, [2017] |
    Series: The church at worship : case studies from Christian history |
    Includes bibliographical references and index.
Identifiers: LCCN 2017031079 | ISBN 9780802873903 (pbk. : alk. paper)
Subjects: LCSH: Public worship—Baptists—History—20th century. | Public worship—Argentina—
    History—20th century. | Baptists—Argentina—History—20th century.
Classification: LCC BX6337 .R88 2017 | DDC 264/.0609820904—dc23
    LC record available at https://lccn.loc.gov/2017031079

Contents

Series Introduction

The Church at Worship offers user-friendly documentary case studies in the history of Christian worship. The series features a wide variety of examples, both prominent and obscure, from a range of continents, centuries, and Christian traditions. Whereas many historical studies of worship survey developments over time, offering readers a changing panoramic view like that offered out of an airplane window, each volume in The Church at Worship zooms in close to the surface, lingering over worship practices in a single time and place and allowing readers to sense the texture of specific worship practices in unique Christian communities. To complement books that study "the forest" of liturgical history, these volumes study "trees in the forest."

Each volume opens by orienting readers to the larger contexts of each example through a map, a timeline of events, and a summary of significant aspects of worship in the relevant time period and region. This section also includes any necessary cautions for the study of the particular case, as well as significant themes or practices to watch for while reading.

Each volume continues by focusing on the practices of worship in the specific case. This section begins with an introduction that explains the nature of participation in worship for ordinary worshipers. Many studies of worship have focused almost exclusively on what clergy do, say, and think. In contrast, insofar as historical sources allow it, this series focuses on the nature of participation of the entire community.

Each volume next presents an anthology of primary sources, presenting material according to the following categories: people and artifacts, worship setting and space, descriptions of worship, orders of worship and texts, sermons, polity documents, and theology of worship documents. Each source is introduced briefly and is accompanied by a series of explanatory notes. Inclusion of these primary sources allows readers to have direct access to the primary material that historians draw upon for their summary descriptions and comparisons of practices. These sources are presented in ways that honor both academic rigor and accessibility. Our aim is to provide the best English editions of the resources possible, along with a complete set of citations that allow researchers to find quickly the best scholarly editions. At the same time, the introductory comments, explanatory sidebars, detailed glossaries, and devotional and small-group study questions make these volumes helpful not only for scholars and students but also for congregational study groups and a variety of other interested readers.

The presentation of sources attempts, insofar as it is possible, to take into account multiple disciplines of study related to worship. Worship is inevitably a multi-sensory experience, shaped by the sounds of words and music, the sight of symbols and spaces, the taste of bread and wine, and the fragrance of particular places and objects. Worship is also shaped by a variety of sources that never appear in the event itself: scriptural commands, theological treatises, and church polity rules or guidelines. In order to help readers sense this complex interplay, the volumes in this series provide a wide variety of texts and images. We particularly hope that this approach helps students of the history of preaching, architecture, and music, among others, to more deeply understand how their interests intersect with other disciplines.

Each volume concludes with suggestions for devotional use, study questions for congregational study groups, notes for students working in a variety of complementary disciplines, a glossary, suggestions for further study, works cited, and an index.

Students of Christian worship, church history, religious studies, and social or cultural history might use these case studies to complement the bird's-eye view offered by traditional textbook surveys.

Students in more specialized disciplines — including both liberal arts humanities (e.g., architectural or music history) and the subdisciplines of practical theology (e.g., evangelism, preaching, education, and pastoral care) — may use these volumes to discern how their own topic of interest interacts with worship practices. Liturgical music, church architecture, and preaching, for example, cannot be fully understood apart from a larger context of related practices.

This series is also written for congregational study groups, adult education classes, and personal study. It may be unconventional in some contexts to plan a congregational study group around original historical documents. But there is much to commend this approach. A reflective encounter with the texture of local practices in other times and places can be a profound act of discipleship. In the words of Andrew Walls, "Never before has the Church looked so much like the great multitude whom no one can number out of every nation and tribe and people and tongue. Never before, therefore, has there been so much potentiality for mutual enrichment and self-criticism, as God causes yet more light and truth to break forth from his word."[1]

This enrichment and self-criticism happens, in part, by comparing and contrasting the practices of another community with our own. As Rowan Williams explains, "Good history makes us think again about the definition of things we thought we understood pretty well, because it engages not just with what is familiar but with what is strange. It recognizes that 'the past is a foreign country' as well as being *our* past."[2] This is possible, in part, because

---

1. Andrew Walls, *The Missionary Movement in Christian History: Studies in the Transmission of Faith* (Maryknoll, NY: Orbis Books, 1996), p. 15.

2. Rowan Williams, *Why Study the Past? The Quest for the Historical Church* (Grand Rapids: Wm. B. Eerdmans, 2005), p. 1.

of a theological conviction. As Williams points out, ". . . there is a sameness in the work of God. . . . We are not the first to walk this way; run your hand down the wood and the grain is still the same."[3] This approach turns on its head the minimalist perspective that "those who cannot remember the past are condemned to repeat it."[4] That oft-repeated truism implies that the goal of studying history is merely to avoid its mistakes. A more robust Christian sensibility is built around the conviction that the past is not just a comedy of errors but the arena in which God has acted graciously.

We pray that as you linger over this and other case studies in this series, you will be challenged and blessed through your encounter with one small part of the very large family of God. Near the end of his magisterial volume *A Secular Age,* Charles Taylor concludes, "None of us could ever grasp alone everything that is involved in our alienation from God and his action to bring us back. But there are a great many of us, scattered through history, who have had some powerful sense of some facet of this drama. Together we can live it more fully than any one of us could alone." What might this mean? For Taylor it means this: "Instead of reaching immediately for the weapons of polemic, we might better listen for a voice which we could never have assumed ourselves, whose tone might have been forever unknown to us if we hadn't *strained to understand it. . . .*"[5] We hope and pray that readers, eager to learn from worship communities across time and space, will indeed strain to understand what they find in these studies.

LESTER RUTH
Duke Divinity School

CARRIE STEENWYK
Calvin Institute of Christian Worship
Calvin College and Calvin Theological Seminary

JOHN D. WITVLIET
Calvin Institute of Christian Worship
Calvin College and Calvin Theological Seminary

3. Williams, *Why Study the Past?* p. 29.
4. George Santayana, *The Life of Reason* (New York: Scribner's, 1905), p. 284.
5. Charles Taylor, *A Secular Age* (Cambridge: Harvard University Press, 2007), p. 754.

Suggestions for Complementary Reading

For students of Christian worship wanting to survey the broader landscape, we recommend using the examples of these volumes alongside other books such as Geoffrey Wainwright and Karen B. Westerfield Tucker's *Oxford History of Christian Worship* (Oxford: Oxford University Press, 2006); Gail Ramshaw's *Christian Worship: 100,000 Sundays of Symbols and Rituals* (Minneapolis: Fortress Press, 2009); Frank C. Senn's *The People's Work: A Social History of the Liturgy* (Minneapolis: Fortress Press, 2006); Martin D. Stringer's *A Sociological History of Christian Worship* (Cambridge: Cambridge University Press, 2005); James F. White's *A Brief History of Christian Worship* (Nashville: Abingdon Press, 1993); and Keith Pecklers's *Liturgy: The Illustrated History* (Mahwah, NJ: Paulist Press, 2012). A brief examination of the myriad aspects encompassing worship can be found in Juliette Day and Benjamin Gordon-Taylor's *The Study of Liturgy and Worship* (Collegeville, MN: Liturgical Press, 2013) or Ruth C. Duck's *Worship for the Whole People of God: Vital Worship for the 21st Century* (Louisville: Westminster John Knox Press, 2013).

For those studying church history, volumes from this series might accompany works such as Mark Noll's *Turning Points: Decisive Moments in the History of Christianity*, 3rd ed. (Grand Rapids: Baker Academic, 2012); Dale T. Irvin and Scott W. Sunquist's *History of the World Christian Movement*, 2 vols. (Maryknoll, NY: Orbis Books, 2001–2012); and Robert Bruce Mullin's *A Short World History of Christianity*, rev. ed. (Louisville: Westminster John Knox Press, 2014).

Students of religious studies might read these volumes alongside Robert A. Segal's *The Blackwell Companion to the Study of Religion* (Oxford: Blackwell, 2006) and Robert A. Orsi's *The Cambridge Companion to Religious Studies* (Cambridge: Cambridge University Press, 2011).

History of music classes might explore the case studies of this series with Tim Dowley's *Christian Music: A Global History* (Minneapolis: Fortress Press, 2011); Andrew Wilson-Dickson's *The Story of Christian Music: From Gregorian Chant to Black Gospel* (Minneapolis: Augsburg Fortress Press, 2003); and Suzel Ana Reiley and Jonathan M. Dueck's *Oxford Handbook of Music and World Christianities* (Oxford: Oxford University Press, 2016).

History of preaching students might study the contextual examples provided in this series along with Hughes Oliphant Old's volumes of *The Reading and Preaching of the Scriptures in the Worship of the Christian Church* (Grand Rapids: Eerdmans, 1998–2010) or O. C. Edwards's *A History of Preaching* (Nashville: Abingdon Press, 2004).

Acknowledgments

We are grateful to the many people who have helped make this volume possible:

» to the missionaries Janet Gerow, Ronald Olson, and Darlene Olson for so graciously sharing their materials with us and allowing us to use them to tell their stories. Their example of faithfulness in Christian service and continued humbleness was evident in how they expressed gladness that their stories could continue to inspire devotion to Jesus Christ. They also exhibited outstanding patience in the years it has taken to bring this volume to print;

» to Andrew Olson, the son of Ronald and Darlene, who helped us make the initial connection to his parents. His offer, coming as part of a chance conversation at church one Sunday, was the trigger that set this whole process in motion. He also was irreplaceable in bringing his familiarity with Argentina into play as he worked with us to create pseudonyms to protect the privacy of the Argentines;

» to the family of Jerry and Janet Gerow, especially Elizabeth Gerow, who helped their mother review initial drafts of this volume and, after her death, worked with us to secure permission to use their family's materials;

» to all the staff at the Calvin Institute of Christian Worship who spent countless hours copying, scanning, typing, translating, and providing other support for this volume, especially María Cornou for her helpful reading and suggestions to make this a stronger, more accurate history;

» to Carrie Steenwyk and John Witvliet, coeditors of this series, who have provided both the initial vision for it and the ongoing impetus for its several volumes;

» to the Lilly Endowment for financial support; and

» to Tom Raabe and Mary Hietbrink for assistance in the publication process.

To any who should be in this list but have been inadvertently left off, we offer both thanks and apologies.

PART ONE

LOCATING THE WORSHIPING COMMUNITY

The Context of the Worshiping Community: Conservative Baptists in Northwest Argentina, Mid-Twentieth Century

Baptist missionary to India and the father of modern missions William Carey famously declared, "To know the will of God, we need an open Bible and an open map." Carey's story and sentiment have long resonated with missionaries serving throughout the world, particularly Baptists. Those representing the North American–based Conservative Baptist Foreign Mission Society (CBFMS) in the middle of the twentieth century were certainly no exception. The CBFMS was born in 1943 through schism within the Northern Baptist Convention, yet just four years later it sent its first missionaries to Argentina to begin training at the Bible Institute of Buenos Aires. In Buenos Aires, the CBFMS partnered with the Christian and Missionary Alliance as well as the Federation of Evangelical Churches of the River Plate. Because early CBFMS missionaries were deeply troubled by what seemed to them a disproportionate number of missionaries in Buenos Aires, they set out to explore the northern regions of the nation; this area would become the mission field for CBFMS missionaries during the next two decades.

Among these church workers were Bob Greenman and C. D. ("Jerry") and Janet Gerow, who entered Argentina in 1948, and Ronald and Darlene Olson, who followed in 1954. Their mission, however, was anything but easy. Even in the middle of the twentieth century, Argentina continued to feel the effects of the 1829 revolution and the political regime of Juan Manuel de Rosas, the influential dictator who ruled the province of Buenos Aires as well as the Argentine Confederation (Confederacion Argentina) from 1835 to 1852. He imposed a colonial system that threatened political liberty across the region. While the latter half of the nineteenth century and the first half of the twentieth century were punctuated by profitable periods, by midcentury the cultural climate had become characterized by national frustration, political instability, and economic fluctuation. Argentina continued to recover from World War II, and Argentines continued to navigate the turbulent and controversial leadership of President Juan Perón. Perón's authoritarian leadership prompted civil unrest, military interference, and ideological tensions that reversed any political and economic progress the country had appeared to make in previous decades.

Argentina's national anxieties were not the only, or perhaps even the most significant, challenge to CBFMS missionary work, however. Competing interests among Catholics and Protestants further complicated the environment for missionary work. Since 1930 the Catholic Church had retained immense political power while Protestants endured one of

The CBFMS believed that little "religious pluralism" existed in Argentina in the first half of the twentieth century, due to the large population of Roman Catholics. CBFMS began ministry in northwest Argentina in the lowland, tropical region east of the Andes Mountains, and this was where the Gerows chose to start their ministry in "letters." The Gerows learned that no formal missions had been established in the nearby foothills of the Andes, so they followed the larger goal of the CBFMS to plant churches in that region.

A conquistador was a leader in the Spanish conquests, especially of Mexico and Peru, in the sixteenth century.

The Plymouth Brethren is a small, conservative, British-originated movement that carried out some of the earliest missionary work in northwest Argentina. It is largely evangelical in character. Seeking to follow the Bible on how to conduct worship meetings, the movement has weekly communion, no classes of lay or clergy, and a restriction against women speaking in worship, among other elements. In Argentina, they were known as Free Brethren, or *Hermanos Libres.*

their most difficult seasons. For instance, under Perón, Catholic education was mandatory in public schools while Protestants were banned from radio stations and had their publications censored. Both groups desired to see their version of Christianity grow, but they did so under significantly different situations. Nonetheless, Protestants worked for the loyalty of the now-independent Argentines with the same competitive, zealous spirit that Catholics did.

Conquistadors had brought Roman Catholicism to Argentina nearly four centuries earlier, and in the ensuing years, numerous priests had contributed to the imprint of a medieval Catholicism that pervaded the Argentine mentality in the mid-twentieth century.[1] In those four centuries, the Catholic Church had its share of successes as well as failures, many influenced by national events, and Catholic practices became deeply embedded in the local and national culture. At times the dominant Catholic culture worked to the missionaries' advantage, but at other times it exposed their vulnerability as Protestants who were also foreigners. Protestant missionaries saw Argentines as a people longing for cultural, political, and religious independence, and they believed the Protestant message of lay leadership, financial freedom, and religious education had the potential to be quite appealing. However, Catholic priests trained in the United States rightly characterized the Protestant missionaries as "pawns in a world ideological struggle."[2]

Beyond the Catholic presence that had permeated Argentine culture for centuries, a stream of Protestant missionaries had also been flowing into Argentina since the late nineteenth century. Among them were individuals from parachurch organizations, such as the Salvation Army and the South American Mission Society, as well as others representing the **Plymouth Brethren**, who first came to Argentina in 1882. The work of these groups served as an important touchstone for the work of all CBFMS missionaries who arrived in the middle of the twentieth century. They also permeated the landscape with beliefs, practices, and ideologies. Some of these were commonly held by Baptists while others were outside the framework of the Baptist missionaries. Nonetheless, Baptists, such as the Gerows, Olsons, and others, possessed a remarkable zeal and a confident determination that they were indeed following the will and the Word of God, and this propelled their work for more than a decade.

The religious climate of Argentina was generally thought to be one of indifference,[3] but the work of CBFMS missionaries in the middle of the twentieth century suggests otherwise. They found pockets of hope in the positive reception they received as they traveled from provinces to cities to villages to *lotes* to homes. The majority of their mission work occurred in farming villages, towns, and communities of northwest Argentina, a region known for its sugarcane, tobacco, citrus, and cattle. There, familiar and pragmatic methods of evangelism

1. Arno W. Enns, *Man, Milieu, and Mission in Argentina: A Close Look at Church Growth* (Grand Rapids: Eerdmans, 1971), 19.

2. Enns, *Man, Milieu, and Mission*, 32.

3. Harwood L. Childs, "The Constitutions of the Latin American Republics," in *Consultation on Religious Liberty in Latin America*, part 2 (New York: National Council of the Churches of Christ in the USA, 1955), 17.

and church planting were widely effective as they traveled by foot, scooter, horse, and rail to establish, visit, or encourage churches, home meetings, and Bible studies. Along the way they played music, handed out tracts, preached, shared the gospel with individuals on the roadside, baptized new believers in ditches and irrigation canals, and held large events at preaching points and tent meetings.

While large public venues were arguably some of the most effective for communicating to large crowds, the most fruitful area of missionary work may have been isolated farming communities where individuals had little or no connection to the Roman Catholic Church; these were places of higher poverty rates and greater social instability than the rest of northern Argentina. Such was true for a former soldier the Gerows recalled in an August 1949 journal entry. While on their way to a meeting by way of a back road rather than the main highway, they met a soldier, living in a shack, who ran after their green truck, waved for it to stop, requested a Bible, and through it found renewed faith in Christ. The Gerows wrote, "God led us down that back road until we found the wandering sheep, who confessed his sin and straying and returned to joy and peace in Christ."[4]

The story of Baptist missionary and father of modern missions William Carey is also perhaps the story of CBFMS missionaries and Conservative Baptists in northwest Argentina in the mid-twentieth century. Armed with a Bible in one hand and a map in the other, they traveled throughout northern Argentina, shared the Word of God, and saw the number of believers in the region grow from about 250 in 1947 to nearly 4,000 by 1967.[5]

---

4. Passage from August 1949, in C. D. Gerow and Janet Gerow, *Letters from Huacalera* (privately published and copyrighted, 1996). This quote is excerpted from this book and is used by permission of the estate of Janet Gerow. No other use or reproduction is allowed without written permission of this estate.

5. Enns, *Man, Milieu, and Mission*, 178.

Timeline

What was happening in the world?	What was happening in Christianity	What was happening in the Argentine church?
		1853: Paving the way for evangelical and Protestant missionaries, Juan Bautista Alberdi advocates the doctrine of religious tolerance in Argentina.
		1860: Religious freedom finally granted to Buenos Aires, meaning Protestants have legal right to worship in Spanish in the entire country.
	1887: A. B. Simpson founds the Christian and Missionary Alliance, which incorporates in 1897.	1882: First missionaries of Plymouth Brethren arrive.
		1889: First missionaries of Salvation Army arrive.
1898: Spanish-American War occurs.		1894: First missionaries of Seventh-Day Adventists arrive.
		1895: First missionaries of Christian and Missionary Alliance arrive.
		1898: First missionaries of South American Missionary Society arrive.
1899–1901: Boxer Rebellion occurs in China.		1899: First missionaries of Regions beyond Mission arrive.
1901: William McKinley is assassinated and Theodore Roosevelt becomes president.	1903: Pope Leo XIII dies, and Pius X is named pope.	
1903: Wright brothers fly first motorized airplane.	1905: Baptist World Alliance is formed during first Baptist World Congress at Exeter Hall in London.	
1906: San Francisco earthquake kills hundreds.	1906: Azusa Street Revival begins in California.	
1912: Titanic sinks after hitting an iceberg.	1910: World Missionary Conference is convened in Edinburgh.	
1914: Panama Canal opens.	1914: Pope Pius X dies, and Benedict XV is named pope.	
1914–1918: World War I is fought.	1914: Assemblies of God Church is formed.	
1916: Hipólyto Irigoyen assumes presidency of Argentina. His first presidency lasts until 1922.		

What was happening in the world?

1919: Eighteenth Amendment to US Constitution is ratified, prohibiting alcoholic beverages.

1920: Nineteenth Amendment to US Constitution is ratified, guaranteeing women the right to vote.

1921: Warren G. Harding assumes presidency of the United States.

1922: Marcelo T. de Alvear, an "heir of conservative liberalism," assumes presidency of Argentina. He rules until 1928.

1923: Calvin Coolidge assumes presidency of United States.

1928: Irigoyen begins second presidency, which will last until 1930.

1929: Herbert Hoover assumes presidency of United States.

1929: October stock market crash creates panic on Wall Street and begins Great Depression.

1930: Argentine Revolution of 1930 influences political and social life in Argentina.

1931: Spanish Republic is formed.

1933: Hitler comes to power in Germany.

1933: Franklin Delano Roosevelt is inaugurated president of United States.

1936: A civil war occurs in Spain.

1941: Japan attacks Pearl Harbor.

1945: Harry S. Truman assumes presidency of United States after Roosevelt dies in office.

1946: Marilyn Monroe receives her first film contract from Twentieth Century-Fox.

1946: Juan Domingo Perón becomes president of Argentina.

1949: People's Republic of China is formed.

1950: Korean War begins.

What was happening in Christianity?

1922: Fundamental Fellowship of the Northern Baptist Convention is formed at a preconvention rally in Buffalo. Out of this group will come the CBFMS.

1922: Pius XI is named pope.

1923: "Militant fundamentalists" from the Fundamental Fellowship of the Northern Baptist Convention form Baptist Bible Union (BBU).

1927: Lausanne Conference is convened.

1932: BBU becomes General Association of Regular Baptist Churches (GARBC)

1943: Moderate fundamentalists split from Northern Baptist Convention to form Conservative Baptist Foreign Mission Society (CBFMS), an agency that would appoint both "liberal and conservative" missionaries.

1946: Members of CBFMS adjust bylaws to make representation contingent upon the funds committed to the Convention.

1947: Conservative Baptist Association of America (CBAA) is formed over complaints of denominational structure.

1947: First Billy Graham Crusade is held in Grand Rapids, Michigan.

1948: World Council of Churches is formed.

What was happening in the Argentine church?

1943: Catholic religious education is required in Argentine schools.

1947: Bob Greenman, the first CBFMS missionary, enters northwest Argentina and evaluates the area.

1948: C. D. ("Jerry") and Janet Gerow enter northwest Argentina as CBFMS missionaries.

1948: Bob Greenman begins active evangelistic work through home meetings and tent campaigns.

1948: A presidential Executive Decree requires that all non-Catholic religious organizations must register with the government.

1949: The Gerows settle into San Pedro and begin missionary work alongside Thomas Easdale.

What was happening in the world?

1952: Maria Eva Duarte de Perón, wife of Juan Perón and more commonly known as "Evita," dies of cancer.

1952: Cost of living in Argentina rises by 40 percent.

1953: Color television introduced in United States.

1953: Dwight D. Eisenhower becomes president of United States.

1954: US Supreme Court ruling in *Brown v. Board of Education* initiates civil rights movement.

1954–1955: Roman Catholic liturgical processions protest Perón's leadership.

1955: Rosa Parks refuses to give up her seat on a bus in Montgomery, Alabama.

1955: Juan Perón is overthrown in a military coup.

1961: John F. Kennedy assumes presidency of United States.

1961: First human space flight.

1963: Kennedy is assassinated in Dallas; Lyndon B. Johnson assumes presidency.

What was happening in Christianity

1950: Name of Northern Baptist Convention changed to American Baptist Convention.

1950: CBAA forms Conservative Baptist Home Mission Society and founds Conservative Baptist Theological Seminary in Denver.

1952: Complete Bible in the Revised Standard Version becomes available.

1954: Evanston Assembly of World Council of Churches occurs.

1955: The Conference of Latin American Bishops (Consejo Episcopal Latinoamericano, or CELAM) is founded and initiates widespread conversation about the mission of the church in Latin America.

1957–1958: International Missionary Council convenes in Ghana.

1958: John XXIII is named pope.

1961: New Delhi Assembly of the World Council of Churches (WCC) occurs, and the International Missionary Council joins council.

1962–1965: Second Vatican Council occurs.

1963: Pope John XXIII dies, and Paul VI is named pope.

What was happening in the Argentine church?

1950: The Gerows hold Easter Conference in San Pedro.

1950: CBFMS missionaries expand into Salta, provincial capital.

1952: CBFMS issues a policy statement encouraging missionaries to create self-sustaining, indigenous congregations. Revisions to this document are made in 1953.

1954: The Gerows move into the village of Huacalera, extending their work into the Andes Mountains bordering Bolivia. This includes the second CBFMS Easter Conference to be held.

1954: Ronald and Darlene Olson enter Argentina as CBFMS missionaries and begin work in Calilegua and Cerrillos.

1954–1955: Processions celebrating the Immaculate Conception of the Virgin Mary and the Corpus Christi in Buenos Aires serve as Catholic protest rallies against Perón.

1955: The Gerows begin work in Ledesma, which includes weekly Bible studies and Sunday celebrations of the Lord's Supper.

1956: The Olsons hold their first Evangelistic Conference in Ledesma on Argentine Independence Day.

1956: CBFMS missionaries expand into San Miguel de Tucumán, a provincial capital.

1957: The Baptist General Conference, envisioning partnerships with CBFMS missionaries, begins work in northern Argentina.

1959–1961: Ronald Olson compiles a list of the fifty-one baptisms he performed, in towns of Prediliana and Libertador.

1962: The Gerows hold their sixth annual Easter Conference in Ledesma; over 500 attend evening meetings.

What was happening in the world?

1964: The Beatles appear on The Ed Sullivan Show.

What was happening in Christianity

1967: Pope Paul VI gives permission for Roman Catholic liturgy to be in the vernacular of a worshiping congregation—rather than in Latin—as part of Vatican II reforms.

1968: Uppsala Assembly of WCC occurs.

1971: Gustavo Gutiérrez coins the term "liberation theology."

1979: Nairobi Assembly of the WCC occurs.

What was happening in the Argentine church?

1962–1964: Argentine Baptists move toward self-sufficiency, as reported by the Gerows; church buildings are constructed without CBFMS impetus or financial support.

1967: The number of Baptists in Argentina exceeds four thousand as a result of missionary work.

Liturgical Landscape

What liturgical world did Conservative Baptists enter in northwest Argentina? If worshipers in northwest Argentina had looked around during the middle of the twentieth century, what might they have seen?

First and foremost, the liturgical world of Argentina was predominately Roman Catholic. Argentina had sustained ties to the Catholic Church for more than four centuries, and worshipers in Argentina were well acquainted with the practices of Catholicism, including the Roman Catholic Mass. In spite of their familiarity with the Mass, Argentine attendance and participation in weekly celebrations were quite low. The best attendance rate occurred in smaller urban areas of the country, but even there only 13 percent attended Mass. Larger urban centers had an even lower attendance rate of 2.3 percent, a number substantially lower than the 17–18 percent average attendance among all of Latin America.[1]

Such low percentages were not the product of any single circumstance, but the combination of several factors. First, until the middle of the twentieth century, bishops and priests conducted the Mass in Latin, rendering it foreign to a culture whose primary language was Spanish. Second, Argentina suffered from a significant shortage of priests, with one priest for every 4,300 Catholics in the country. Third, priests and bishops known as "religious radicals" among Catholics became involved in political struggles, particularly those against President Perón in 1954–1955, and this further alienated individuals from the church.[2]

Though there was often distaste between Catholics and Protestants in Argentina, these and other challenges increased Argentines' receptivity to Protestant Christianity, as did the more egalitarian, **free church** worship practices CBFMS and other Protestant missionaries carried into the country. For an overview of mainline Protestant worship in Argentina in the twentieth century, see Wilhelm Wachholz, "Mainline Protestants in Latin America," in *The Oxford History of Christian Worship*, ed. Geoffrey Wainwright and Karen B. Westerfield Tucker (New York: Oxford University Press, 2006), 651–60. To read about Baptist worship, see Christopher J. Ellis, *Gathering: A Theology and Spirituality of Worship in Free Church Tradition* (London: SCM, 2004). What Pentecostal and charismatic worship may have offered the Argentine community, in theology and other benefits, can be found in Teresa Berger and Bryan D. Spinks, eds., *The Spirit in Worship—Worship in the Spirit* (Collegeville, MN: Liturgical

---

1. Arno W. Enns, *Man, Milieu, and Mission in Argentina* (Grand Rapids: Eerdmans, 1971), 32–33.
2. Enns, *Man, Milieu, and Mission*, 32–33.

Press, 2009). See also Simon Chan, *Liturgical Theology: The Church as Worshiping Community* (Downers Grove: IVP Academic, 2006).

Worshipers attending a Catholic Mass in Argentina in the middle of the twentieth century would have felt the same hierarchy that was present in the Catholic Church in Rome. Latin Americans became frustrated with this hierarchy because they believed it looked solely to the interests of the powerful and the elite. To read more about the hierarchy of the Roman Church and the challenges it faced in Argentina, see Justo L. González, *The Reformation to the Present Day*, vol. 2 of *The Story of Christianity* (San Francisco: HarperOne, 2010), 520–25.

However, the frustrations with Catholic hierarchies were secondary to the political, economic, and other cultural challenges the twentieth-century Argentine church faced. All these forces gave rise to a native Argentine Catholicism in the first half of the twentieth century characterized by new liturgical practices, beliefs, and theologies. This is often known as **liturgical inculturation**, described well in the work of Anscar J. Chupungco, *Liturgical Inculturation: Sacramentals, Religiosity, and Catechesis* (Collegeville, MN: Liturgical Press, 1992). For instance, to compensate for the shortage of priests in the country, religious radicals began authorizing laymen to conduct Mass when priests were unavailable, translating Scriptures into Spanish, and setting the Mass to Argentine folk music after Vatican II. For a general overview of contextualizing religious music, see C. Michael Hawn, "Part III Regional Perspectives: An Introduction to Caribbean, Central and South American Hymnody," in *New Songs of Celebration Render: Congregational Song in the Twenty-First Century*, ed. C. Michael Hawn (Chicago: GIA Publications, 2013), 262–80. A specific case study of one Argentine's contextualization of Latin American hymnody can be read in C. Michael Hawn, *Gather into One: Praying and Singing Globally* (Grand Rapids: Eerdmans, 2003), 32–71.

Challenges the Argentine Catholic Church experienced were not uncommon; they were prevalent throughout the global Catholic Church. Innovators demanded change and cried for the church to keep up with modern times, while traditionalists fought to maintain the status quo. In 1962, Pope John XXIII convened the Second Vatican Council (Vatican II) to address challenges facing the Catholic Church at large. For a general overview of Vatican II and its placement in the larger liturgical renewal movement of the twentieth century, see Frank Senn, *Christian Liturgy: Catholic and Evangelical* (Minneapolis: Augsburg Fortress, 1997), 629–37. Vatican II, which met from 1962 to 1965, instituted significant changes in the global Catholic Church, a number of which were specific to the Catholic liturgy. For an overview of these changes, see André Haquin, "The Liturgical Movement and Catholic Ritual Revision," in *The Oxford History of Christian Worship*, ed. Geoffrey Wainwright and Karen B. Westerfield Tucker (New York: Oxford University Press, 2006), 696–720.

Liturgical changes were addressed in one of the council's first documents, *Sancrosanctum Concilium* ("Constitution on the Sacred Liturgy"), released in December 1963. This document initiated some of the most significant changes in the Catholic liturgy since the Council of

Chupungco is an influential Roman Catholic liturgical scholar who has studied worship and culture. His work is particularly helpful for understanding the liturgical narrative of Baptist missionaries in Argentina.

Trent (1545–1563), including provisions that enabled "full, conscious, and active participation" in the Mass by all worshipers. It formally sanctioned practices that religious radicals had begun at a grassroots level, such as conducting Mass in the local language with indigenous music, but it also paved the way for these indigenous practices to become more prevalent in places where they were lacking. For an overview of how such indigenous practices evolved throughout the twentieth century in Catholic worship, as well as in other denominations, see John R. K. Fenwick and Bryan D. Spinks, *Worship in Transition: The Liturgical Movement in the Twentieth Century* (New York: Continuum, 1995). According to Mark Noll, Vatican II joins the Edinburgh Missionary Conference (1910) and the Lausanne Congress on World Evangelization (1974) as three twentieth-century turning points in Christianity, particularly within the United States. All three gatherings influenced, directly or indirectly, the work of CBFMS missionaries and Argentine Baptists. See Mark Noll, *Turning Points: Decisive Moments in the History of Christianity*, 3rd ed. (Grand Rapids: Baker Academic, 2012), 261–306.

While the liturgical scene in Argentina was predominately Roman Catholic, it also included Protestant worship practices from nineteenth- and twentieth-century missionaries; pagan beliefs, customs, and practices native to Argentina; and an intense popular religiosity. A general overview of the religious climate in Argentina in the middle of the twentieth century can be found in Arno W. Enns, *Man, Milieu, and Mission in Argentina: A Close Look at Church Growth* (Grand Rapids: Eerdmans, 1971). The mixture of beliefs and competition of ideologies in twentieth-century Argentina has been described as "Christo-paganism," a syncretism of Christian, pagan, and popular beliefs and practices. To add to this complexity, Argentina itself was an amalgamation of individuals and groups of various European backgrounds, Indians, **mestizos**, and more. The cumulative effect of Argentina's culture was that worshipers encountered a combination or blend of these influences, and all religious leaders—particularly CBFMS missionaries—had to make critical decisions, liturgical and otherwise. For an overview of how cultural complexities impacted Latin American worship in the twentieth century, see Miguel A. Palomino and Samuel Escobar, "Worship and Culture in Latin America," in *Christian Worship Worldwide: Expanding Horizons, Deepening Practices*, ed. Charles E. Farhadian (Grand Rapids: Eerdmans, 2007), 107–30.

Sociologist Andrew Walls provides a helpful backdrop for understanding how the CBFMS missionaries may have approached decisions in the field. Walls identifies two prominent principles in Christian mission movements: the "indigenizing principle" and the "pilgrim principle." Neither has been immune to critique, but Walls claims each is congruent with practices found in the four Gospels. The indigenizing principle focuses on accepting people as products of a specific time and place, while the pilgrim principle acknowledges a global Christianity with dual citizenship in the world and the kingdom of God. Walls's pilgrim principle is useful for understanding CBFMS missionaries' work, particularly their transmission of worship practices in Argentina. The missionaries carried worship practices they

Mestizos are people of mixed European and indigenous non-European ancestry.

knew into Argentina, adapted them in light of Argentine culture, yet retained continuity with the broader Christian tradition. See Andrew F. Walls, *The Missionary Movement in Christian History: Studies in the Transmission of Faith* (Maryknoll, NY: Orbis, 1996), 7–9. To read further about decisions worshipers and worship leaders face in cross-cultural environments, see Kathy Black, *Culturally-Conscious Worship* (Saint Louis: Chalice, 2000). See also Justo L. González, ed., *¡Alabadle! Hispanic Christian Worship* (Nashville: Abingdon, 1996).

While the liturgical landscape in Argentina was complex, so, too, was the broader landscape of missions in the twentieth century. Liturgical scholars studying worship on the mission field must be aware of the relationship between the missionaries' sending culture and the natives' indigenous culture; this topic formed the core of conversations about **missiology** in the twentieth century. Were missionaries, products of the sending culture, to reject, adopt, or reframe the native culture, beliefs, customs, and practices as they worked to develop a Protestant culture? And, how would their decisions impact their work, of which worship was only a small part? For a comprehensive overview of Protestant missions and missiology in the twentieth century, see David J. Bosch, *Transforming Mission: Paradigm Shifts in Theology of Mission* (Maryknoll, NY: Orbis, 1991), 368–510.

Missiology is the study of the principles and practices of religious missions, particularly those within Christianity.

Some mission agencies and missionaries have been criticized for the methods and practices they used to accomplish their tasks, but Robert Woodberry has provided an alternative narrative for missionary work by "conversionary Protestants." His sociological research underscores the importance of Protestant missionary work for being a catalyst for the political and economic development associated with democratic nations. See Robert D. Woodberry, "The Missionary Roots of Liberal Democracy," *American Political Science Review* 106, no. 2 (May 2012): 244–74. In retrospect, foreign missions during the nineteenth and twentieth centuries have contributed significantly to the rise of Christianity in the Global South. Philip Jenkins illustrates how Christianity's "center of gravity" shifted during the twentieth century from the Global North to the Global South. "If we want to visualize a 'typical' contemporary Christian, we should think of a woman living in a village in Nigeria, or in a Brazilian *favela*," notes Jenkins. See Philip Jenkins, *The Next Christendom: The Coming of Global Christianity*, 3rd ed. (New York: Oxford University Press, 2011), 1–3. His work also illustrates the impact of Protestant missions as various nationalities (such as American and Argentine) commingled and adapted Christianity to specific contexts. For instance, the biblical theology espoused by many missionaries from the Global North has been described as conservative and even **fundamentalist**, yet circumstances in the Global South prompted new converts to find Scripture socially liberating—a characteristic not usually present in fundamentalist traditions. See Philip Jenkins, *The New Faces of Christianity: Believing the Bible in the Global South* (New York: Oxford University Press, 2008), 178–93.

Woodberry defines "conversionary Protestant" missionaries as those who actively attempt to persuade others of their beliefs, emphasize lay vernacular Bible reading, and believe that grace/faith/choice saves a person, not group membership or sacraments. All three qualities characterize the missionaries represented in this volume.

A fundamentalist is someone who upholds a strict and literal interpretation of Scripture. This term as an adjective describes such an approach to the Bible.

Geographical Landscape

This map shows northwest Argentina around 1950. The areas in which the CBFMS missionaries worked are outlined in black. As you look at the map, imagine the complex geography in which the missionaries worked: mountains, valleys, rural areas, and cities.

Cautions for Studying Argentine Baptist Worship History

Readers should be aware of some methodological difficulties they may encounter when studying the worship of Conservative Baptist missionaries in northwest Argentina at the middle of the twentieth century:

- Firsthand accounts of worship by the missionaries in Argentina represent only one aspect of their mission work. The CBFMS missionaries were there, first and foremost, to follow the Great Commission by spreading the gospel of Christ. While liturgical practices were a component of their work, they were not the only component, nor were they the most important component. This mentality of liturgical practice is prevalent among Baptists.
- The cumulative picture of worship among these Baptists is pulled from descriptions derived from missionary journals over an extended period of time. Baptist worship does not follow a prescribed order or sequence; therefore, to study Baptist worship practices one relies on a series of descriptions that pull from practices that seem to be standard over a period of time—the source in this case is the nearly twenty years of journals created by CBFMS missionaries.
- While Baptist worship is conducted in an orderly fashion, printed orders of worship that reflect sequencing and the relationship between each liturgical event rarely exist. This is true for the Baptists in Argentina.
- Baptist worship does not use liturgical books. Prayers, testimonies, and other elements are often extemporaneous. Because of this, there is a scarcity of liturgical texts to study.
- Only outlines of the sermons are available; full sermon manuscripts are not. Readers do not know everything that was said in the sermons, and this leaves a significant gap theologically, culturally, and pastorally.
- While texts to the songs that Argentine Baptists sang in worship are available, no recordings exist. Therefore, we don't know what the music sounded like. For instance, what was the instrumentation? How fast or slow was the music sung? How was it taught? Were all stanzas of hymns sung, or just the first and last? Was the congregational music loud and robust and highly participatory, or was it primarily soft and passive?
- Baptism records exist, but they primarily emphasize the number baptized and in what towns they were baptized. Little sociological data exists about the baptized individuals, such as age and gender.

- Since the Baptist missionaries were focused on a onetime, personal decision to declare Jesus Christ as Savior and Lord, little data exists about the spiritual maturation process that might have occurred through worship and discipleship.
- Worship happened in church buildings, in tents, and in open air. This spatial variety implies that the particular worship environment was not important, and it makes it difficult to know exactly how each liturgical space was used and arranged.
- Only a few photographs remain of worship and other liturgical events from the CBFMS missionaries, and not all of them contain sufficient captions, dates, and locations to decipher their content. This makes it difficult to determine the "who, when, where, why, and what" of worship, as well as how worship changed over short and long periods of time.
- Because animosity often existed between the local Catholics and the foreign missionaries, it can be difficult to determine how much their work overlapped, if at all, under the larger umbrella of Christianity rather than within the denominational umbrellas of "Catholic" and "Baptist."
- It is tempting to characterize all Argentine Baptist worship according to the records of the Olsons. However, given the number of other Baptist and Protestant missionaries present in northwest Argentina, such assumptions may well be incorrect or inaccurate. For instance, if the Plymouth Brethren maintained a presence in Argentina throughout the twentieth century, how might their worship practices have differed from those of the Baptists? If Methodist or Presbyterian missionaries were in Argentina, how might their worship practices have differed from those of the Baptists?
- Many of the relevant documents pertaining to the worship practices of CBFMS missionaries are in private, family-owned collections. What is available is limited and pieced together through oral histories, which makes formulating a comprehensive understanding nearly impossible.
- With a few exceptions, the available sources to tell the history of these Christians in northwest Argentina come from the white American missionaries. Having narrative accounts from their Argentine and Bolivian immigrant parishioners would provide a fuller history, but such accounts are not readily available.
- Current missiology is much more aware of cultural sensitivities, racial dynamics, and ethnocentrism than was the case a half century ago. And current readers might share the same awakened awareness. Thus a modern reader, realizing the difference in time, might need to be patient with now-questionable statements in order to utilize the primary sources as historical sources, especially when those sources provide basic factual information otherwise unobtainable. The challenge is to balance this patience with legitimate critique of questionable attitudes of the past.

Significant Themes and Practices to Observe

As you study the following materials, be on the lookout for these significant themes and practices that are categorized by primary elements in worship.

Piety

- A strong emphasis is placed on a personal decision to take Jesus Christ as one's Savior and Lord. This process occurs by personally repenting of sin and surrendering to the work of Christ in one's life. Christian baptism—often accompanied by the individual's personal **testimony**—follows.
- As evidenced in preaching and personal reading and study, Scripture is held in high regard as the sole source of authority.
- Evangelism was the primary focus of the missionary work in Argentina, and Baptists there did whatever they could inside and outside of worship to increase the number of converts. While evangelism has looked different in various times and places, in this context it often included both a personal approach, such as handing out tracts to individuals in the market or on the roadside, and a populist approach, such as conducting large tent meetings as part of a massive crusade.
- In contrast to Roman Catholicism in Argentina, which emphasized religion as an act to be performed through attending Mass and receiving the sacrament, Baptist piety was first and foremost a personal experience. It was connected to the individual's inward disposition that flowed outward into worship and mission.
- Argentine Baptists valued autonomy in worship and congregational governance. The Baptist ecclesiology, then, with its flexible worship practices and loose structure, allowed local and regional traditions and customs to take root and flourish.

Giving a **testimony** (in other words, testifying) is speaking about how one has experienced the grace of God, especially the saving work of Jesus Christ.

Time

- Time was more relaxed in Argentine society than in American society, and this had an effect on the Argentine church. Worship was structured, but worshipers and leaders were not constrained by a strict time schedule.
- The week included multiple gatherings, each of which had a distinct purpose. The main worship gathering was held on Sunday morning, and it included a weekly observance of the Lord's Supper; this was retained from the Plymouth Brethren influence.
- Sunday evenings were reserved for evangelistic services, the pinnacle of the congregation's liturgical life, because their primary purpose was to give individuals the opportunity to be saved. These services often included music, testimonies, and preaching, but the climax was an altar call where individuals had the opportunity to profess their faith publicly in the worshiping community.
- In addition to these two Sunday services, the congregation gathered midweek for a prayer meeting and on Saturday evenings for a group Bible study.
- While Argentine Baptists did not follow the same liturgical year and festivals as the Roman Catholic Church, three annual events were important to their liturgical life: a Christmas Eve service, an **Easter Conference,** and an annual evangelistic campaign. Each of these included elements important to Baptist worship in the United States as well as Argentine culture.

Pan de Navidad is a festive dish made from various ingredients such as chocolate, raisins, fruits, and almonds.

- The Christmas Eve service, for instance, included a children's program, common to missionaries from the United States, as well as *pan de Navidad* (nativity bread) and cool refreshments—necessary for a country south of the equator, whose Christmastide occurs during summer.
- The Easter Conference included multiple evening evangelistic rallies that were well attended because they paralleled Holy Week services in the Roman Catholic Church, held at the same time. Their popularity can be attributed to Argentine participation in Catholic Holy Week services prior to "conversion" to a Protestant faith. Evening Easter Conference rallies were more popular than sunrise services, which were *not* well received by Argentines, who were accustomed to late nights and late mornings! The Easter Conference, however, conflicted with Catholic practices of penitence and fasting during Lent and Holy Week.
- The annual evangelistic campaign the Baptists held mirrored Billy Graham Crusades that were popular at the time. The campaign's multiple services occurred outdoors over extended evenings and periods of time.

Place

- While the CBFMS missionaries worshiped in church buildings and in some instances helped construct permanent fixtures, where they worshiped was one of the least important factors.
- Worship occurred wherever "two or three or more were gathered" in the name of Jesus Christ. This might have been in a set time in a church building or tent, but it could just as easily happen impromptu in a house, field, train, truck, or road when believers felt the need to sing, pray, or testify.
- Mobile fixtures, such as tents, were important for the itinerant Baptist missionaries, and they became important symbols of the missionaries' evangelistic campaigns, rallies, and work.
- Baptisms often occurred in irrigation ditches, canals, or any pool of water deep enough for baptism by immersion. The people would often gather near the water while the minister administered baptism to the candidate.
- Church buildings, tents, and other physical locations filled to capacity were important signifiers of efficacy. That is, when a physical space reached capacity or overflow status, it was an important sign that the Spirit was working through the CBFMS missionaries in the hearts and minds of the Argentine Baptists whose souls needed to be saved.

A common Baptist way to suggest that immersion baptism is necessary is to decipher the original Greek word in the New Testament ("baptize" = "immerse") and to look at the accounts of baptism that speak of immersion in a substantial body of water, either literally (e.g., John 3:23; Mark 1:10; Acts 8:38) or figuratively (e.g., Rom. 6:4; Col. 2:12).

Prayer

- Prayers were almost always in Spanish. This was a significant contrast to prayers performed by Catholic priests, which were in Latin.
- Prayers were almost always extemporaneous. In mid-twentieth-century Baptist spirituality, a spontaneous prayer was more sincere, or "from the heart."
- Such spontaneous communication between the individual believer, the gathered community, and Jesus Christ was important for the American missionaries who advocated for the priesthood of all believers. This connected well with Argentines who desired to express thoughts, feelings, and devotions personally as opposed to going through a Catholic priest.
- Argentine Baptists commonly used scriptural fragments, paraphrases, or whole verses in their prayers to indicate that they were familiar with the Word of God.

Most Baptists insist that all who believe in Jesus Christ as Savior and Lord are priests. In other words, ordained and lay ministers in the church are to be considered equal. 1 Peter 2:5 is often cited as the touchstone for this important distinctive of Baptist polity.

Preaching

- Preaching among Argentine Baptists changed according to the specific meeting. For instance, a Sunday morning sermon may have related to a topic of Christian discipleship and living, while a Sunday evening sermon at an evangelistic rally may have centered on sin, the need of all people to repent, and the saving power that comes only through Christ.
- Baptist missionaries would have certainly preached in any of the services, but in their quest to establish local and autonomous congregations, they also encouraged the Argentine believers to preach or give testimonies.
- Education figured prominently in helping the Argentines understand the preaching they heard. Because literacy was on the rise in Argentina, Baptist missionaries could assume members of their congregation had read or would read and study the Word of God outside of worship. Thus, preaching was also a form of teaching about Scripture, and this teaching would often inform personal Bible study practices between times of worship.
- The egalitarian leadership from the pulpit would have presented a stark contrast to Catholic practices, which were largely dominated by ordained clergy. Another contrast would have been worship in the native tongue; until the mid-1960s, Catholic Argentines would generally have heard only Latin in the Roman Mass.

Music

"Evangelical" refers to a kind of Protestant Christianity characterized by evangelism, personal experiences of conversion, and an emphasis on the Bible as the key authority for individuals and churches. Gospel hymns came from white, nineteenth-century congregational songs and often emphasized personal experience of God and salvation.

Choosing music spontaneously during extended periods of singing was typical among Plymouth Brethren in Argentina, and this Conservative Baptist practice might represent a continuity with the Brethren.

- Songs used in most Baptist congregations were typical **gospel hymns** that would have been well known to North American **evangelicals**. Most of them were written in the late nineteenth or early twentieth century.
- The texts of the most common hymns among the Ledesma Baptists were christocentric, and most of them have themes of repenting from sin and returning with a renewed personal devotion to Christ.
- A number of worship choruses, written by Argentine Baptists, were also used in worship. For instance, CBFMS missionary Ronald Olson compiled a songbook of music composed by the congregation in Salta, whose songs have similar themes to gospel hymns: professing faith in Jesus Christ and knowing him as personal Savior.
- As is common in Baptist worship, a musician often chose the music rather than a preacher. The music may have been chosen spontaneously, and there were often extended periods of singing where music was chosen at random by members of the congregation.
- True to Baptist worship around the world, congregational singing for the Argentine Baptists developed a strong sense of Christian community and fellowship.

- A variety of small ensembles often provided special music for worship and in other gatherings. This might have been a men's quartet or women's trio singing a new song, or a familiar song done in a new fashion. Such special music was seen as a musical offering, in contrast to a financial offering, though it did not replace the latter! It was also a common practice in evangelical worship at the time, prominently modeled through the Billy Graham Crusades.
- Instruments were also used when available. These may have included a trumpet, a portable organ, and other brass instruments.

People

- C. D. ("Jerry") and Janet Gerow and Ronald and Darlene Olson were missionaries from North America with the Conservative Baptist Foreign Mission Society. They, along with other missionaries from the CBFMS as well as other Protestant agencies, served in northwest Argentina during the middle of the twentieth century.
- The Gerows and Olsons ministered in small, rural towns and villages full of sugarcane workers; sugarcane is one of the prominent agricultural crops in the area. These workers and their families could have been of European descent, or they could have represented local ethnicities such as the Guaraní and Quechua (i.e., Amerindians). It was common for the sugarcane workers to embrace Christianity with their whole family, and oftentimes, with their friends. These Amerindians were often the first and most ready respondents to the Baptist missionaries. Ministry and evangelism among the American Baptists became communal experiences for these Argentine farmers.
- The cultural dynamics for the Baptist missionaries were not simple or one-dimensional. In addition to their own culture shifts in moving from America to a remote part of Argentina, they were negotiating the particular social and multicultural dynamics of the area. Northwest Argentina at the time was not only occupied by Argentines of various European ancestries but also by Amerindians, many of whom were Bolivian immigrants who had come for work. The latter were often very poor and subject to exploitation by the economic system, including the sugarcane plantations.
- The Argentines were generally very family oriented and generationally focused.
- The number of believers in the area where CBFMS missionaries worked was approximately 250 when they entered in 1947. Nearly twenty years later, the number had grown to an estimated 4,000 because of their work and emphasis on evangelization.

PART TWO
Exploring the Worshiping Community

Describing the Community's Worship: Conservative Baptists in Northwest Argentina, Mid-Twentieth Century

*What follows is a description of the worship by congregations formed through the evangelistic work of a group of Conservative Baptist Foreign Mission Society (CBFMS) missionaries, C. D. ("Jerry") and Janet Gerow and Ronald and Darlene Olson, in northwestern Argentina in the years just after World War II. Both couples possessed a focused commitment to share the gospel in order to make new disciples for Jesus Christ and create new churches from these converts. And both had a deep evangelical and Baptist commitment to the Bible as the center of Christian life and the church. With these commitments, they worked hard to plant new Baptist churches. Their congregations sought to distinguish themselves from an entrenched Roman Catholicism on the one hand and an insurgent **Pentecostalism** on the other, all the while laboring diligently to overcome reservations people had about Baptist Christianity.*

Armando Morales[1] stood alone in the desert, high in the arid Andes Mountains of northwest Argentina near his home, reading Bible passages out loud at the top of his lungs.

Very odd behavior. What accounts for it? Well, drunkenness and drug abuse had sent Morales's life careening out of control. They had driven his wife out of his home, back to the mountain village where she had grown up. His son, who had worked with Morales in his carpentry shop, had left him, too. His downward spiral had even affected the quality of his work to the point where he could no longer make decent furniture. Armando Morales had become a desperate man.

One day an agent serving with the Argentine Bible Society offered Morales a Bible with the promise that reading it would change his life. Morales took the book, eagerly grabbing the opportunity. He began to read the Bible, but nothing changed. He decided that he was not reading it loud enough, unaware that it was not volume but faith that mattered. That's when this lonely carpenter went out to the desert to shout Bible passages. But that didn't work either. Something must be wrong with this book, he thought.

Then he met Jerry Gerow, a Baptist missionary who was selling Bibles acquired from a colporteur, a traveling Bible vendor. Morales sat Gerow down and complained that something was defective with his Bible. The missionary explained that the sheer act of reading was not the point. Instead, the Bible had power because it testified to a Savior, Jesus Christ. Using

---

1. To protect the privacy of the individuals and their descendants, pseudonyms for Argentines have often been used.

the same Bible that had become a symbol of frustration for Morales, the Baptist evangelist unfolded the gospel through a series of verses until the Argentine carpenter was led to an opportunity to surrender to the carpenter from Nazareth, Jesus. Gerow told the Argentine that this Savior was clapping at the door of his heart, waiting for Armando Morales to invite him in. This the Argentine did.

Argentines in small towns or rural areas announce their arrival at a home by clapping their hands, not by knocking on the door or ringing a doorbell.

Janet Gerow (left) leading an Argentine woman in a one-on-one Bible study

Source: personal photograph of the Gerow family. Used by permission of the estate of Janet Gerow. No other use or reproduction is allowed without written permission of the estate.

Starting in the mid-twentieth century, scenes like this conversion were commonplace for the missionaries of the Conservative Baptist Foreign Mission Society (CBFMS) serving in the farthest northwest provinces of Argentina. Twin emphases on Jesus Christ as Savior and the Bible as the only reliable guide to experiencing the salvation offered through him characterized this work. Armed with these convictions, a growing number of CBFMS missionaries came from the United States and spread through the area's towns, villages, and farming-related communities to evangelize. They used a variety of means to declare Christ as Savior, always eager to gain converts from whoever would respond to the gospel message, including those willing to come from Roman Catholic backgrounds, whether nominal or active. This goal of evangelizing persons—rather than performing some kind of social service—was at the heart of these missionaries' sense of vocation.[2]

Is any such missionary effort even proper? Some historians have argued that mission was the deputy of Western colonialism and that these movements combined to exploit or destroy indigenous culture. Others have suggested that Christian mission's relationship to indigenous culture is more complicated.

2. Lamin Sanneh, for example, speaks of an inherent tendency toward translation of Christianity into the vernacular language and culture, meaning that Christian missions both bring into a culture and receive out of a culture. Look for where these Americans must set aside their American presuppositions to engage the Argentine culture and receive from the Argentine people. In what ways did a new form of Baptist faith arise? See Lamin Sanneh, *Translating the Message: The Missionary Impact on Culture* (Maryknoll, NY: Orbis, 1989).

The focus on Jesus Christ as Savior and the Bible as the ultimate guide to this salvation also shaped the gathering of these new converts into local churches. The Baptist missionaries were commissioned not merely to make new disciples, but to gather them into churches that were self-led and self-propagating in terms of continuing commitment to personal evangelism. The Bible and Christ remained central in the life of these churches and in the piety of the new believers. They read the Bible,[3] studied it, memorized it, and distributed it in order to grow closer to Christ, who had died to save them, and in order to introduce family and acquaintances to this Savior.

Not surprisingly, the worship at these churches evidenced the same emphases. Consider the central role of the Bible in worship, for instance. Reading and preaching the Bible were some of the most important features of a service. Extemporaneous acts like praying and testifying to one's experience of salvation, too, were sprinkled with biblical quotes and allusions. And, following long-standing Baptist sensibilities, finding a scriptural precedent or command was important for knowing what to do in worship and how to do it. Baptism of believers by immersion only is perhaps the most obvious example of this sentiment. Similarly, the Baptists' worship was saturated with Christ as Savior. Worship's content, for example, was tethered to rehearsing Jesus Christ's ability to save people from sin and to appeals to believe in this gospel. All these practices show recurring characteristics of Baptist worship and, even more broadly, those strands of Protestantism that can be labeled free church or evangelical.

Armando Morales's story also hints at the role of cultural adaptation by the Baptist missionaries, who worked hard on evangelizing and planting churches in the context of northwest Argentina. For example, Gerow did not simply repeat a biblical image (of Christ knocking on the door; see Rev. 3:20) to Morales but culturally interpreted it in a way that had meaning for the Argentine. Contextualization appears on a more subtle level in this incident, too, in the use of an intermediate agent who had connections to the remote mountain villages of the Andes. To succeed, an American missionary could not have simply paraded in and begun evangelizing. Rather, a missionary would have to find a person who already had connections to the village people. The Argentine context is seen also in Morales's presuming that sheer performance of religious acts sufficed. Missionaries were constantly leading converts away from that presumption, as they struggled against a popular form of Roman Catholicism that saw religion as outward action.

Jerry Gerow's efforts in the mountains of northwest Argentina were not the only kinds of Conservative Baptist missionary work in the area. Indeed, the extension into the arid Andes

---

3. That push is likely in light of evangelical mission work elsewhere, as noted by sociologist Robert D. Woodberry. He has found that Protestant missionaries often were central to expanding formal education because they wanted people to read the Bible in their own language. This push was a common contribution missionaries made, sometimes inadvertently, to the rise of democracies in colonies and former colonies. See Robert D. Woodberry, "The Missionary Roots of Liberal Democracy," *American Political Science Review* 106, no. 2 (May 2012): 244–74.

A Plymouth Brethren missionary, Charles Kirby Torre, allegedly introduced tent meetings in the late nineteenth century. Soon other Protestants replicated the practice.

followed earlier endeavors of the CBFMS in the towns and farming villages at the foot of the mountains.[4] The first CBFMS missionary, Bob Greenman, had evaluated the region at the end of 1947; he was attracted by how little Protestant presence there was in the area. It was not a completely virgin field, however, in that the Plymouth Brethren, a small British-based church, had planted several churches since the beginning of the century. That the remaining Brethren missionaries, like Thomas Easdale, were aging and eager to find someone to take over their work heightened the region's appeal. In 1948, Greenman began active evangelistic work, using home meetings and tent campaigns, which were to become common methods for the Baptists.

Ronald Olson and one of the Argentine Baptists stand outside the first worship space in Ledesma, which was a room in the house of a believer. The sign indicates the service times: Wednesdays, Saturdays, and Sundays at 8 p.m.; the Lord's Supper at 9 a.m. on Sundays; and Sunday school at 10:30 a.m.

Source: personal photograph of Ronald Olson

4. For history of the work, see [Conservative Baptist Foreign Mission Society], *Founded on the Word, Focused on the World: The Story of the Conservative Baptist Foreign Mission Society* (Wheaton, IL: Conservative Baptist Foreign Mission Society, 1978), 47–50; Hans W. Finzel, ed., *Partners Together: 50 Years of Global Impact; The CBFMS Story, 1943–1993* (Wheaton, IL: Conservative Baptist Foreign Mission Society, 1993), 151; Arno W. Enns, *Man, Milieu, and Mission in Argentina: A Close Look at Church Growth* (Grand Rapids: Eerdmans, 1971), 96–99.

Over the next several decades, the number of CBFMS missionaries (most of the American names in the material that follows are of these missionaries) continued to expand, as did the number of Baptist converts and churches. Within two years of Greenman's arrival, the CBFMS team in the region numbered eleven, which included Jerry and Janet Gerow, who had arrived in 1948 and settled into the town of San Pedro for missionary work early in 1949. Expansion continued through the 1950s and 1960s. Ronald and Darlene Olson arrived in 1954 and began work in farming communities like Calilegua and Cerrillos before establishing themselves in Ledesma, a community associated with a large sugarcane plantation. The CBFMS missionaries' work went beyond their cities of residence to a multitude of villages and towns largely associated with the farming that dominated the area. Thus the missionaries ministered in churches, preaching points (occasional places to preach), and house groups scattered throughout the region. From an initial core of about 250 believers inherited from the Plymouth Brethren work, the number of Baptists in the region had grown to over 4,000 by 1967.[5] Understanding the geography of northwest Argentina helps us understand how the missionaries worked. Imagine this area of mission work as roughly shaped like a Y. (See the map on p. 14.) The upper right arm and the lower base were the areas first evangelized: the hot, subtropical lowlands that rested at the base of the Andes Mountains. The region was a lush farming area specializing in sugarcane production. Rain clouds that approached the area dropped all their moisture at the foot of the mountains; the Andes squeezed the clouds dry like a sponge. The missionaries worked in established towns like Jujuy (pronounced Hu-hu-ee), San Pedro, and Libertador as well as in a variety of *lotes* (plantation villages) across this farming region (except for Jujuy, all in the upper right part of the Y). Eventually the work extended down the base of the Y to cities like Salta (1950) and Tucumán (1956), both provincial capitals. Throughout the lower part and right side of the Y, the Baptists traveled the roads and railroad lines, spreading tracts, establishing Bible studies, preaching, and evangelizing.

The second phase of the Baptist missionary effort—expansion in the mountain villages of the Andes—began with the Gerows' move to Huacalera (pronounced Hwa-ca-le-ra) in 1954. This extension was to the upper left arm of the Y. From Jujuy, which is on the base of the imaginary Y's left arm, the Pan-American Highway inched up the Andes until it entered Bolivia to the north. (Huacalera was a village on this highway.) Unlike the fertility of the first region, the Andes were severely arid. Off the main highway, mule trails and unimproved roads led to mountain villages like Santa Ana and Palca de Aparzo. Bit by bit, Baptist evangelism spread to the villages off the highway, especially to the area to the east (the area between the arms of the Y).

Knowing the geography and the region's economy also helps make sense of the diversity of peoples the Baptist mission sought to reach. The agricultural lowlands (that is, the base

Ledesma adjoined the city of Libertador General San Martín, so that Ledesma and Libertador (meaning "liberator" in English) are somewhat interchangeable names.

An initial investigation in 1952 found that no formal mission ministry had been established in the northwestern Andean region toward Bolivia. In 1953, the Gerows looked for accommodations in villages at about eight or nine thousand feet above sea level, in order to better access other villages located even higher. In late 1954, they rented a house in Huacalera, in the foothills of the Andes and ideally located on the highway between the provincial capital, Jujuy, and the Bolivian border.

5. Enns, *Man, Milieu, and Mission*, 178.

and right arm of the imaginary Y), reflecting the ethnic diversity of Argentina as a whole,[6] were a greater ethnic melting pot than one might imagine.

Four groups lived in the towns and farming communities. One was the people of European backgrounds. These came from a variety of European countries and included folks of distant and recent immigration, especially from Italy and Spain. These people, strongly nationalistic, forceful in their commitment to Argentine culture (sometimes including a cultural attachment to the Roman Catholic Church), and often of higher economic classes, were the least receptive to the Baptist work. Other people groups were more receptive, including mestizos and two indigenous groups, the Guaraní (pronounced Hwa-ra-nee), originally from the tropical regions of Argentina, Uruguay, and Paraguay, and the Quechua (pronounced Ketch-wa), a mountain-based tribe. Many of the mestizos and Quechua were Bolivians who had immigrated to Argentina to find work in agriculture. These Bolivians proved to be one of the most responsive groups for Baptist evangelization.

Mountain communities, the area encompassed by the second phase of the Baptist mission, were more isolated and not as diverse ethnically. In the Andes the communities had experienced less demographic turnover or expansion. The long-standing residents were Quechua or mestizo, by and large. Because the mountain folks were often suspicious of outsiders, the Baptist missionaries had to take a more indirect, subtle approach to evangelization, using intermediaries who already had connections with the people. Another distinction was how whole villages sometimes converted together, following the decision of village leaders. In addition, the Roman Catholic presence was sometimes more sporadic in the mountain communities in that priests came only for occasional visits and did not reside in the communities.

Loved by some and hated by others, Perón governed during a time of extreme political polarization in Argentina. Many praised his efforts to eliminate poverty and dignify labor, while others considered him a demagogue willing to use violence and other means to quell opposition from left-wing and conservative opponents.

Whether cutting sugarcane in hot fields or laboring in small artisan shops in the mountains, all the people in Argentina lived in a country racked with political and economic instability in the mid-twentieth century. The CBFMS work began during the tumultuous presidency of Juan Perón, who ruled from 1946 until 1955, when he was unseated by a military coup. Perón's presidency and the times that followed were so turbulent that one historian said Argentina during this period was "consumed by political divisions as profound as any throughout its history."[7] Because Argentina's government was a strongly federal system, any change of national government shook the structure of daily life all the way down to who delivered the mail. Despite the political tumult, however, the increase during Perón's regime in the number of students in public schools and in the sheer number of schools in more remote parts of the country like northwest Argentina produced great benefits for Baptist

6. Enns, *Man, Milieu, and Mission*, 97–98.
7. David Rock, *Argentina, 1516–1982: From Spanish Colonization to the Falklands War* (Berkeley: University of California Press, 1985), 262.

evangelization in the form of widespread literacy. Baptist missionaries could rely on new and potential converts being able to read the Bible directly.

Coupled with the political instability was economic turbulence.[8] In 1952 alone, the cost of living rose by 40 percent. Between 1946 and 1955, the money in circulation increased eightfold whereas production only inched upward. Removing Perón did not stabilize the country's economy. The people experienced a recurring series of severe cycles of economic growth and decline. The constant was chronic inflation, which was averaging 30 percent a year by the early 1960s.

The political turmoil touched the country's religious landscape, too, as the national government was involved in church affairs. For the Baptists, that meant keeping an eye on rules for entering the country and conducting their religious work. Changing government rules also impacted the constant backdrop of the Baptist work: the role of the Roman Catholic Church in Argentine society. Initially, Perón's presidency looked like it meant the further ascendancy of the Catholic Church. For instance, he had rewarded the church's support with legislation in 1947 making Catholic religious education compulsory in schools. But eventually the relationship cooled as Perón reversed some of the earlier indulgences he had granted the church. Catholics responded by using their outdoor liturgical processions on feast days in the church calendar to make political statements against Perón.[9] For example, the 1954 procession celebrating the **Immaculate Conception of the Virgin Mary** (December 8) and the 1955 **Corpus Christi** procession in Buenos Aires were huge rallies protesting Perón. The latter came after Perón had announced plans to introduce a constitutional amendment to establish a formal separation of church and state. Devoted Catholic clergy and laypeople surely felt as if the church was losing its traditional place in Argentine culture, making them even more wary of losing parishioners to Baptist incursions.

To such Catholics, Baptist worship seemed a different world with conflicting values and practices. And it was. The ministry in Ledesma led by Ronald Olson is an example of the worship of the Conservative Baptist church. Notwithstanding small variations across the breadth of the CBFMS work in northwest Argentina, this church was fairly representative of the other Conservative Baptists in the region. Moreover, the Ledesma church's worship reflects some basic characteristics of Baptist and free church worship generally.

One point of reflection concerns the basic elements that make up most worship services: Scripture readings, prayers, a sermon, and interspersed congregational songs (originally psalms; today often special music by smaller ensembles, including choirs). These have been the most recurring elements in Baptist services globally.[10] Include the occasional testi-

Think of the challenges that this economic reality would have caused, especially in light of this mission society's desire for its new congregations to be self-sustaining. Imagine this reality in light of "A Study of Indigenous Policies and Procedures" found on 115–40.

Olson's congregations shared several characteristics in congregational singing with the Plymouth Brethren in Argentina.

8. See Rock, *Argentina, 1516–1982*, 265–321.

9. Rock, *Argentina, 1516–1982*, 315.

10. Christopher J. Ellis, *Gathering: A Theology and Spirituality of Worship in Free Church Tradition* (London: SCM, 2004), 43.

mony, confession of sin, or special media presentation, and one has the key building blocks that made up the majority of services for Ledesma's Baptists. In addition, there was often little concern to provide strict thematic cohesion between the different parts of a service. It was not uncommon for the songs to be chosen by a musician rather than the preacher, for instance.[11]

In Ledesma, the reason for a lack of cohesion in the service was often more basic: extended time could be spent in allowing people to spontaneously choose songs or small ensembles to provide special music. Many times these ensembles were not scheduled to sing or did not know they would be singing when the service began, but the fluid nature of the service created opportunities to include them. Indeed, the special music could so threaten to get out of hand that a discerning worship leader had to be careful to prevent this.[12]

The Baptist church in Ledesma had multiple worship services every week, each with a slightly different balance of the elements listed above. The midweek evening service was mainly a prayer meeting. After some songs and a short message perhaps, most of the time was spent praying extemporaneously. This type of prayer was standard; these Baptists had few, if any, written prayer texts for worship. Everyone who wished could pray. (Extemporaneity and spontaneity often go hand in hand in Christian worship.) A Saturday evening service had a stronger emphasis upon the study of the Bible. Prayers, songs, and other elements of congregational participation could be added as thought appropriate. The Sunday morning service would have included all the elements listed above as well as a weekly celebration of the Lord's Supper. This practice of weekly communion is rather exceptional in Baptist worship history. The Baptists in Ledesma did so as a carryover from the church's roots in the earlier Plymouth Brethren work in the region. Ronald Olson would have introduced the Supper with a message on the cross or some aspect of Christ's saving self-giving along with material drawn from 1 Corinthians 11 (the Lord's words as the scriptural warrant for having the Supper and a warning not to receive it unadvisedly). Sometimes, prior to receiving communion, an Argentine Baptist's seriousness about not displeasing and offending God moved him or her to confess sin before the entire congregation.[13]

The worship week culminated with a Sunday evening evangelistic service, meaning that the songs and sermon were on elementary Christian topics like sin, repentance, faith, and salvation. Although the whole mission was shot through with evangelism, the emphasis of this service would have been aimed at anyone who had not surrendered to Christ to be saved.

---

11. Ellis, *Gathering*, 57.

12. Ronald Olson, email to Lester Ruth, December 16, 2006. I am much indebted to several email correspondences from Rev. Olson for the details of this description of Ledesma's worship.

13. Olson, email to Ruth, February 25, 2006. Olson notes that the Baptist practice of "fencing the table" was not as strict as that of the Plymouth Brethren, who would publicly prohibit nonmembers from the table or refuse to service them. After warning that persons should examine themselves before communion (see 1 Cor. 11:28), the Ledesma Baptists left it as a self-examination.

In contrast to this evening service, that day's morning service would have covered topics more enriching for the church as a whole and for believers to grow in their faith, for example, sanctification and holy living.

Several annual celebrations supplemented weekly worship. On Christmas Eve, a service of special songs, choir pieces, poems, and dramas lasted several hours. There was widespread participation by adults and children alike, contrary to the initial expectation of the American missionaries, who had envisioned a children's program like what they knew in the United States. The service ended with refreshments of cold pizza, soda pop, sandwiches, and *pan de Navidad* (nativity bread), an Italian fruitcake with little fruit.

The Easter Conference was an even bigger annual worship event. It began on the Thursday before Easter and continued through Easter night. The conferences were regional events, drawing Baptists from the area churches. (Multiple conferences could be conducted by CBFMS churches simultaneously.) Services with a strong evangelistic appeal to nonbelievers were held each night. The Roman Catholic influence on the culture meant that the **Good Friday** services were the most attended because everyone already expected special worship activities on that day. Services for believers and children were held in the morning and in the afternoon, with appropriate emphases for growing as a follower of Jesus Christ. On Easter Sunday morning, there was a communion service. Although some missionaries tried to introduce sunrise services, these services generally were not well received.

The Easter Conferences were often occasions for tension between the Baptists and Roman Catholic clergy. Some of the Baptist celebratory practices conflicted with Catholic rules on fasting during the season. And the traditional Catholic liturgical processions on Good Friday seemed to inevitably bump into the Baptist meetings. On perhaps no other day were the two contrasting approaches to Christian worship on such public display. The disparity was obvious.

The other big annual event was the evangelistic campaign. Using a tent and a variety of means of proclaiming the gospel, the Ledesma Baptists took to public arenas to seek new evangelical believers in Jesus Christ. Multiple services were held with a strong emphasis on inviting nonbelievers to repent and surrender to Christ. The techniques, sometimes drawn from American revival practices (e.g., Billy Graham Crusades), included soloists, choirs, multimedia presentations on Christ (films and slides), and sermons by outside evangelists.

Although the worship of the Ledesma Baptists provides insight into the nature of Baptist or free church worship more generally, its particular contextual flavor should not be overlooked. One background factor that shaped Ledesma's worship was the influence of the prior Plymouth Brethren work in the region. Having weekly communion is perhaps the most notable example in that Baptists elsewhere, even in other parts of this same Argentine work, tend to receive the Lord's Supper less frequently. But the Brethren influence also can be seen, perhaps, in the regular use of lay leadership or in the tent meetings of the Ledesma Baptists. The Brethren roots for the latter we have already noted, and that group's practice, too, could

In Argentina, which is south of the equator, Christmas occurs during the hottest time of the year.

Is it surprising that Catholic influence on the culture still shaped some Baptist practices? Good Friday commemorates the crucifixion of Jesus Christ.

set the stage for how often Baptist lay members were called upon to pray, preach, testify, and conduct other acts of worship. But the practice should not be solely attributed to Brethren influence, since it often is found elsewhere among Baptists.

Similarly, the region's culture shaped how Ledesma Baptists worshiped. A culture's influence on worship has both obvious and subtle aspects. An example of an obvious influence would be the language used in worship, which was Spanish in Ledesma. But culture impacts how a congregation worships in less obvious ways, too, such as the use of the body, sensibility to time, the arrangement and use of space, the manner of making music, the manner of preaching and praying, and dominant metaphors and images. How these factors combined to subtly shape Ledesma's worship meant that Baptist worship there would not be quite like Baptist worship in another region or country, even in other Spanish-speaking areas. Recognizing that fact can keep one from presumptions or caricatures about Ledesma's worship.

In several important ways the culture itself did shape these Baptists' worship. One was how education, both formal and informal, molded the people. The high rates of literacy meant that the Baptist predilection for close attention to the Bible found ready roots among the people. Close attention by every believer to Bible passages characterized how they studied, evangelized, and worshiped. Having people make direct connections to God's Word was critical. Education also created enhanced speaking skills among the people. They were used to having to demonstrate new knowledge by speaking it. Thus, when Baptist worship gave them the opportunity to participate by testimony, prayer, or preaching (in contrast to the clergy-dominated leadership of Roman Catholic worship), the people were ready.

The Bolivian immigrants, Quechuas and Guaranís, spoke Spanish as a second language, specifically, as the language of Spanish colonialization. The worship of the surrounding Catholic parishes would have been in Latin until the reforms of the Second Vatican Council took hold in the 1960s.

By and large, this clergy domination would not change for Roman Catholics until after Vatican II, if at all.

Following other North American evangelicals, CBFMS missionaries sometimes used sets of Bible verses strung together to lead someone to faith in Jesus Christ. The accounts by the Baptists indicate several, including the two below. One can imagine how the missionaries could bring someone to a point of decision to trust Christ by discussing the Scriptures in these sequences. The New International Version of the Bible is given below, although the Baptists' evangelization would have been done in Spanish.

Here is one trajectory:

- *John 1:12*   *Yet to all who received him, to those who believed in his name, he gave the right to become children of God.*

- *John 3:16*   *For God so loved the world that he gave his one and only Son, that whoever believes in him shall not perish but have eternal life.*

- *John 3:18*   *Whoever believes in him is not condemned, but whoever does not believe stands condemned already because he has not believed in the name of God's one and only Son.*

- **John 3:36**   *Whoever believes in the Son has eternal life, but whoever rejects the Son will not see life, for God's wrath remains on him.*

- **John 5:24**   *[Jesus said:] I tell you the truth, whoever hears my word and believes him who sent me has eternal life and will not be condemned; he has crossed over from death to life.*

- **John 10:5**   *But they will never follow a stranger; in fact, they will run away from him because they do not recognize a stranger's voice.*

Here is another sequence:

- **Romans 1:16**   *I am not ashamed of the gospel, because it is the power of God for the salvation of everyone who believes: first for the Jew, then for the Gentile.*

- **Romans 3:23**   *All have sinned and fall short of the glory of God.*

- **Romans 6:23**   *The wages of sin is death, but the gift of God is eternal life in Christ Jesus our Lord.*

- **Romans 10:9–10**   *If you confess with your mouth, "Jesus is Lord," and believe in your heart that God raised him from the dead, you will be saved. For it is with your heart that you believe and are justified, and it is with your mouth that you confess and are saved.*

- **Romans 10:13**   *Everyone who calls on the name of the Lord will be saved.*

Another area of cultural impact was the ethos of the worshiping community. This church in Ledesma valued frugality and simplicity in worship. The size and scope of the worship did not have to be grand or professional to be considered good. The worship, like much of the church's life, arose out of a common bond of Christian fellowship, meaning worship was a grassroots effort that crossed generations. It was not merely for some professional staff to lead while the church watched.

Likewise, being in Argentina shaped a congregation's sensibility to what was the appropriate use of time liturgically. Once worshiping, the Ledesma congregation was engaged in a service where time was fluid. Strict adherence to time schedules was not the practice. Although flexible, the worship was orderly, with a sense of progress.

Cultural appropriateness for this congregation's worship was made easier by a couple of factors. One was the CBFMS's commitment to an "indigenous" method in establishing churches. (See p. 116.) The CBFMS believed that the New Testament approach to mission

The fittingness of worship for the specific people who are worshiping became a worldwide, dominant theme of worship history in the late twentieth century. Labeling this concern "liturgical inculturation" is common among Roman Catholics and some Protestants.

meant developing local congregations that were "self-supporting," "self-governing," and "self-propagating." Although the written policy did not explore liturgical inculturation per se, the more general value of having the means for a congregation's long-term viability arise from within the people, not imported from outside, would seem to open a CBFMS-originated congregation to indigenous ways of worshiping.

Worship traditions in which there is a common liturgical text for an entire denomination potentially have less flexibility with respect to inculturation.

That this was a *Baptist* mission reinforced this approach to liturgical inculturation. Unlike some traditions with set prayer texts and universal practices that the missionary must seek to introduce and appropriately adapt, the free church approach to Protestant worship, from which Ronald Olson and the other Baptist missionaries came, had no set texts other than the Bible and no prescribed order of worship other than what could be deduced from Scripture. Baptist polity, which emphasizes the integrity of each local congregation, likewise contributed to how these Baptists approached worship. Cultural adaptation can flourish with this type of liturgical flexibility.

The worship of the Argentine Baptists reflected their own specific context, but it also mirrored to some degree the nature of Baptist worship more generally. This reflection of Baptist worship extended to specific practices and to the general liturgical ethos, especially the four main qualities identified by Baptist scholar Christopher Ellis. The two primary values in this ethos are attention to Scripture and the importance of personal devotion by the worshiper.[14] The first involves both the reading and preaching of the Bible in worship and the root commitment that God should be worshiped in ways appointed by means of biblical example or mandate. Nothing carries the same weight of authority for determining worship as the Scriptures, especially the New Testament. How do Christians know how to worship? Search the Scriptures, and do what can be found there to be a clear example or command; reject that which does not have biblical support or is contrary to the Scriptures.[15]

This use of the Bible reinforces the Baptist confidence that scriptural worship is divinely appointed, not human invention. From the human perspective, the corresponding value is obedience to the command of God.[16] But Baptists, whether in Ledesma or elsewhere, would never intend for worship to be merely rote obedience or outward performance. Thus, a Baptist approach to worship emphasizes the importance of a worshiper's devotion. As Christopher Ellis notes, this theme is "actually a cluster of concerns, including a concern for personal faith, a devotional openness to the Holy Spirit, and a valuing of sincerity and religious experience."[17] Outward obedience is not enough, although it cannot be neglected. A worshiper's proper

14. Ellis, *Gathering*, 74.

15. For application of this principle generally in the Baptist approach to Christianity, see R. Stanton Norman, *The Baptist Way: Distinctives of a Baptist Church* (Nashville: Broadman and Holman, 2005), and L. Russ Bush and Tom J. Nettles, *Baptists and the Bible*, rev. ed. (Nashville: Broadman and Holman, 1999). The principle is not limited to Baptists; another historical example would be the Puritans of the seventeenth century.

16. Ellis, *Gathering*, 76.

17. Ellis, *Gathering*, 74.

inward disposition and faith are crucial. This would be a critical distinguishing mark for what the Baptists perceived in Roman Catholic worship.

> Several scholars have sought to define the qualities that characterize evangelicalism generally. Consider how the following definitions apply to the Argentine Baptist mission. D. W. Bebbington spoke of the "marks of Evangelical religion" being conversionism, the belief that lives need to be changed; activism, the expression of the gospel in deeds; biblicism, a particular regard for the Bible; and crucicentrism, a centeredness on the sacrifice of Christ on the cross. Similarly, George Marsden identified the essential evangelical beliefs as the final authority of the Bible; the real historical character of God's saving work recorded in the Bible; salvation to eternal life based on the redeeming work of Christ; the importance of evangelism and missions; and the importance of a spiritually transformed life.

These first two values—attention to Scripture and personal devotion—highlight the Baptist approach to baptism. Baptists call it an ordinance, not a sacrament, in that the reason to do baptism is to obey the command or ordinance of the Lord. The emphasis is placed on Christ's command to be baptized and on biblical examples of full immersion as the scriptural mode of baptism. The emphasis is not placed on the sacrament bringing about salvation in the one baptized. Rather, it is an act of obedience to the Savior whom one has already accepted by faith. It is an identifying mark of a believer and, therefore, of the church as a visible assembly of believers. Therefore Ronald Olson taught new Argentine Baptists that rituals like baptism are wonderful if they are about relating to Christ by faith, but are simply dead without a prior relationship with Christ.[18]

> Thus, by definition, baptizing infants is excluded. But what about small children who can speak for themselves? Determining the age at which one can be baptized can be an interesting pastoral issue for some Baptists.

Two further values normally characterize Baptist worship; both are seen in the Argentine worship.[19] One is the emphasis on the integrity of the local congregation. It *is* the church of Jesus Christ. The local congregation is a normative expression of the body of Christ. One need not look to larger regional or denominational structures. Use of worship resources produced beyond the local congregation is voluntary. The second is the forward- or upward-looking dimensions of Baptist piety. These dimensions are seen in the concern with an individual's ultimate hope and destiny, as well as a concern to use church discipline to make the church a pure bride for Christ, to use a biblical image. These dimensions also serve as the impetus for praying in worship for those who do not know Christ and for the zeal for evangelism.

> Forward-looking would emphasize the coming kingdom of God; upward-looking would emphasize enjoyment of heaven. Both deal with the question of ultimate human hope and destiny.

It would be difficult to overemphasize the place of Christ and evangelism in the worship of Argentine Baptists. Jesus Christ as the Savior sent by God to find sinners was the recurring

18. Olson, email to Ruth, January 4, 2007.
19. Ellis, *Gathering*, 90, 95.

The Baptist work in northwest Argentina continues today, although it is no longer dependent upon foreign workers. The churches are generating their own indigenous pastors and leaders, and have even sent a missionary couple to another continent. Although many of the first Baptist converts were Bolivian immigrants suffering racial persecution and segregation and doing manual agricultural labor, their children are often respected leaders in schools, government, medicine, and media.

theme of worship, whether in song, testimony, prayer, or sermon. His was the redeeming face of God. These Baptists did not use generic talk of God but celebrated the many facets of how Christ loved and saved them, especially in his atoning death. Many of the songs remembered Christ as Savior. Some songs celebrated the Savior as the reason to praise God, and other songs lifted up Jesus as Savior to invite others and call them to decision. Similarly, the phrases used to describe when someone had been saved tended to have a strong Christ element in them. The Baptists thus spoke of surrendering to Christ, giving their hearts to him, receiving him, coming to him, accepting him, knowing him personally, and finding victory in him.

Not surprisingly, a commitment to individual evangelism is pervasive throughout the written material available from the Argentine Baptists. Both the experienced missionaries and the rank-and-file Baptist converts, if faithful to their common vocation, actively sought to lead others to know the Lord Jesus Christ. This divine drama played out as much in the streets and homes as it did in the church assembled for worship on Sunday. Again and again, the missionaries sensed God's providence in this work. God the Father's guiding hand and the Holy Spirit's mysterious labor combined in ways that brought people and gospel together at the right moment so that people could believe in Christ for salvation. This providence was sometimes apparent only after the fact, but the Baptists trusted in it nonetheless as they kept up their witness to a crucified and risen Savior. With this trust, the Baptists were free to use a wide variety of means (tracts, individual and group Bible studies, outdoor services, etc.) to evangelize.

Corporate worship was not exempt from the divine drama of evangelism. The Baptists knew from their own experience that worship could be part of God's providential arrangement to reach a person. Thus the commitment to evangelize carried over into worship. It was obvious on those occasions when special evangelistic services were held, as noted above. It was also clear in the use of audiovisuals in worship to portray Jesus Christ. **Flannel graphs**, movies, and 35mm slides helped the people visualize Bible stories, especially the life of Christ. Evangelism was also evident in how sermons usually ended with an invitation for persons who had never surrendered to Christ to repent and believe that Jesus had died for their sins.

A flannel graph is a presentational tool that uses felt characters/objects and a felt backdrop. The felt adheres to itself, allowing easy manipulation of the characters and objects to tell Bible stories.

Indeed, the Baptists of northwest Argentina would have been disappointed if anything they did failed to raise the fundamental issue: "Will you believe? We have a book that tells of a Savior who can change your life." This book—and the gospel it contained—was the solution for desperate people.

Documenting the Community's Worship

PEOPLE AND ARTIFACTS

Jerry Gerow Outside Tent

One of the regular yearly practices of the Baptists of northern Argentina was extended evangelistic services in tents. Here Jerry Gerow (far right) stands outside the tent used for the evangelistic rally in August 1948 in the town of San Pedro in the province of Jujuy. The sign indicates that services will be held all week at 9 p.m. each day.

Source: C. D. Gerow and Janet Gerow, *Letters from Huacalera* (privately published, 1996), p. 108.

Darlene Olson and Other Women Singing

Darlene Olson (far right) sings with another American missionary, Evelyn Hatcher (middle), and an Argentine Baptist, Elsa de Rios, in a tent meeting during the annual Easter campaign. The placement of special musical pieces in the order of worship, whether by soloists, small ensembles, or choirs, was a common practice in evangelical Protestant (and Baptist) worship in the period. The sign on the tent wall evokes an Easter theme: Christians rising with Christ to the heavens (probably based on Ephesians 2:6).

Source: personal photograph of Ronald Olson. Used by permission.

Argentine Woman Who Offered Her Home for Worship Meetings

Maria Bustamante was one of the first Baptist Christians from Ronald Olson's missionary work. Before a church was built, she offered her home for worship meetings.

Source: personal photograph of Ronald Olson. Used by permission.

Ronald Olson with Ledesma Baptists

Ronald Olson poses with some of Libertador's/Ledesma's Baptists in the 1950s. They stand outside the site for a new church.

Source: personal photograph of Ronald Olson. Used by permission.

Sociedad Bautista Evangélica
REPUBLICA ARGENTINA

SOCIEDAD MISIONERA BAUTISTA CONSERVADORA DEL EXTERIOR INSCRIPTA EN EL FICHERO DE CULTOS BAJO EL NUMERO 212

BAUTISMOS

Nov. 29, 1959
1. Pablo Lozano   Prediliana
2. Leonidas de Lozano   "
3. Emilio Herrera   "
4. Antonia de Herrera   "
5. Natalia, viuda de Diaz   "

April 10, 1960
6. Domingo Cruz   Maiz Negro
7 Leucardia Yurquina   "   "

May 1, 1960
8. José Luna   Libertador
9. Manuel Mendoza   "
10. Rosalía, viuda de Martinez

May 25, 1960
11. Cecilia Mariano   Maiz Negro
12. Falta nombre   2
13. Falta nombre   "
Felipe Antonio   14   Elena

May 29, 1960
15 Manuel Cardozo   Libertador
16. Bautista Cardozo   "
17. Isabel de Luna   "

Sin Fecha
18. Carlos Gonzalez   Cañitas
19. Celestina Aramayo   "
20. Isabel Vaca   "

September 1960 (25th)
21. Mercedes de Silva   Libertador
22. Francisco Silva   "
23. Ramona de Orrillo   "

Nov. 13, 1960
24. Ramona de Cardozu   "
25. Cornelio Mamani   "

Nov. 27, 1960
26. Ana de Diaz   Prediliana
27. Martina Herrera   "
28. Ambrosio Gallardo   "

Dec. 25, 1960
29. Jorge Diaz   Prediliana
30. Lucinda de Diaz   "
31. Jacinto Segovia   "

May 6th, 1961
32. Segundo Juarez   Libertador
33. Ramona Olivera   "
34. Juana Delgadilla   "

May 25, 1961 La Bajada
35. Estevan Choque
36 Feliciano Choque
37. Domingo Arce
38. Armando Varga

May 28, 1961 Libertador
39. José
40. Angel Vegas
41. Maria Carrizo
42. Isabel Carrizo
43. Margarita del Valle Carrizo

August 6, 1961
44. Julia Rodriguez de Jarma
45. Benjamin

Oct. 29, 1961 Libertador
46. Victor Ramos   Predil.
47. Domingo de Ramos Predil.

Dec 31, 1961
48 ...
49. Maria Lydia Bustamante
50. ...
51. ...

* POR QUE DE TAL MANERA AMÓ DIOS AL MUNDO, QUE HA DADO A SU HIJO UNIGENITO. PARA QUE TODO AQUEL QUE   *
  EN EL CREE NO SE PIERDA, MAS TENGA VIDA ETERNA' SAN JUAN 3:16

List of Baptisms Starting in 1959

Ronald Olson compiled the following list of baptisms he performed from November 1959 to December 1961. In that time he baptized fifty-one persons in the towns of Predili-ana, Maiz Negro ("black corn" in English), and Libertador (the town also known as Ledesma).

Source: photograph by Lester Ruth of article owned by Ronald Olson. Used by permission.

Hand-Driven Record and Record Player

The CBFMS missionaries emphasized personal evangelism in their work. The hand-driven record player was one of the means used to introduce the Argentines to the gospel and call for their response in faith to Christ. Easily folded and transported, it was brought into homes, where possible converts could hear the good news about Jesus Christ and his death to save. This record player dates from a little later period than the era covered in this book, although at that time tracts, films, and filmstrips were used for the same purpose.

Source: photograph by Lester Ruth of record player owned by Ronald Olson. Used by permission.

Worship Setting and Space

Construction of Church

The CBFMS's policy advocated self-reliance in newly created churches. This included the financing and construction of buildings. Here native Baptists work together to construct a separate church building in the town of Libertador (or Ledesma). Previously the Baptists in that city had met in homes, until a believer gave them a room of his home for worship. Although additions have been made, the building under construction in this picture is still in use.

Source: personal photograph of Ronald Olson. Used by permission.

Jerry Gerow with People Outside Church

Jerry Gerow (far right) stands with the Baptist congregation of Humahuaca in the province of Jujuy. The sign over the door says Evangelical Baptist Temple in Spanish.

Source: C. D. Gerow and Janet Gerow, *Letters from Huacalera* (privately published, 1996), 208.

National Pastor Baptizing in Ditch

Baptisms in irrigation ditches were common among the Argentine Baptists. In this photograph, an Argentine pastor, himself an earlier convert of the Baptist mission, administers the ordinance (the preferred term for Baptists, rather than "sacrament") while the church watches from the banks of the ditch. This baptism shows the Conservative Baptist mission's desire for the cultivation of native leadership as well as such classic Baptist emphases as baptism by full immersion.

Source: personal photograph of Ronald Olson. Used by permission.

Communion Service

Unlike most Baptists through history, the Baptists in northwest Argentina celebrated the Lord's Supper every week. This shows the influence of the Plymouth Brethren who had first evangelized the area. (Plymouth Brethren had weekly communion.) Here Libertador (or Ledesma) Baptists sing in anticipation of receiving the Supper, which rests under the linen cloths on the table.

Source: personal photograph of Ronald Olson. Used by permission.

Arid Mountains

In October 1954 Baptist missionaries Jerry and Janet Gerow extended their Argentine work into villages in the arid Andes Mountains along the border of Bolivia. This terrain contrasted with the lush agricultural valleys where the work started and where Ronald and Darlene Olson continued to minister.

Descriptions of Worship

Jerry and Janet Gerow's Accounts of Their Missionary Activities in the Agricultural Lowlands from 1948 through 1953

The following excerpts are from the prayer letters and family correspondence of C. D. (Jerry) and Janet Gerow composed for their supporters in North America. Missionaries typically write such letters to keep informed those who pray for and give to their ministries. The accounts begin with the Gerows' arrival in the country and the development of their ministry in the agricultural regions of northwest Argentina up to 1954. Sometimes the writer is Jerry Gerow and sometimes Janet Gerow. The excerpts were selected to show the nature of evangelism, church planting, and worship in this part of Argentina.

From time to time the missionaries show the cultural and ethnic complexity of their nascent missionary work as they negotiate not only their migration to a new, Spanish-speaking environment but also the economic and racial diversity of the area.

May 21, 1948—We are a block and a half from a huge convent. . . . After our street meeting a couple of weeks ago, there appeared 2 or 3 foot letters, painted on the wall, "WE DON'T WANT THE PROTESTANTS. ARGENTINA IS A CATHOLIC NATION." . . . Oh well, we aren't looking around us, but up. He will give us grace and strength, and protection to do what He has planned for us here. We are praising Him for many chances to witness!

August 21, 1948—The trip was interesting, miles and miles of scrubby trees and cactus of all kinds, endless salt flats with no foliage at all, great areas with no sign of human life, and vast prairies and deserts with a few cattle wandering around, etc. How the cars sway on a narrow gauge railroad! We had a 21 car train, behind a little British engine. Up here there is so much sugar cane for miles in all directions.

August 29, 1948—(CDG [Jerry Gerow] on train to B[uenos] Aires)—The Tent Campaign was great! About 50 decisions for the Lord. I played the portable organ for song service, trumpet in brass trio, sang in vocal trio, etc. (All possible without perfect Spanish yet!) Had big open air meeting last Sunday in the square by the R. R. Station. About 300 heard the message. I was struck by how much the Indians in the north are like the Navajos, among whom we worked in AZ & NM [Arizona and New Mexico]. An old British gentleman, Thos. Easdale, has spent 33 years here doing missionary work among them, has cried and prayed for help for years without avail, and is thrilled that we (CBFMS) are working here.

October 1948—A presidential Executive Decree requires that all non-Catholic religious organizations, personnel, meeting places, and meetings, must be registered with the government. Each must possess a receipt, or virtual license, in order to function. No meetings without this "Comprobante." No new work or meetings may be started without previous application for recognition, etc.! Pray that the Lord may raise up a strong, trained, spiritual national leadership, for the days of the foreign missionary in this land may be numbered. The story of redeeming love must be spread until Jesus comes!

February 28, 1949—We moved into our house in San Pedro last Wednesday, and have been going steady ever since. We're nearly unpacked! The Carnaval (each February) Conference slowed us down. God has worked in the meetings. We saw lives changed, broken homes restored, families reunited, folks repenting and making things right, etc. Uncle Tom and I baptized 26 in the irrigation ditch. A great group of Indians gathered on the banks, and the bridge, to join in the joy of that hour. Many eyes were filled with tears, as we listened to the testimonies of those who had found salvation and victory in Christ, and were now confirming it in this step of total dedication. It was something to do all this in Spanish, but I was able to express what was in my heart correctly, thank the Lord.

April 26, 1949—We had a prayer and business meeting last night (every Monday night), and finally divided the field responsibilities formally. To date it has been "hit or miss," or Easdale sort of ran everything, because he always had before we arrived. Janet and I will be responsible for Mira Flores, San Antonio, El Puesto, and Mendieta. The first three are plantation settlements on the Leach Estates (British Sugar Company with headquarters, offices, and refinery at La Esperanza). San Antonio work was started by Easdale and is where we have about 60 in a Bible class every Thursday. Mira Flores and El Puesto have no work, and we are praying for wisdom for beginning. We have done preliminary visitation there.

Mendieta presents a real challenge! It is an entire Sugar Company, with many workers' settlements or *lotes* (where administrators and laborers live) all over the place. It probably represents a population of 3000–4000 souls, plus hundreds more during harvest. The center

Several of the regular features of the Baptist missionary work can be seen here: use of tents, use of available musical instruments, a variety of musical expressions, and a call for individual decisions. None of this was completely new in the United States or Argentina. Plymouth Brethren had been using tents in this mission. Thomas Easdale was an elderly Brethren missionary.

This October 1948 decree was during the first presidency of Perón, when he was very close to the Catholic Church.

This Carnaval Conference was a Plymouth Brethren tradition, held annually since 1910.

Notice Gerow's gratitude for being able to minister in Spanish. Statements like this remind us that the Gerows and the Olsons were working in a new country, culture, and language, and their viewpoint naturally reflected an American ethnocentrism. But, bit by bit, they got to know their new environment from the inside out.

is about 10 miles from San Pedro, on the road to the provincial capital. We would have to obtain permission to begin on that company's property, and the priest is already there with his chapel, etc. Pray with us.

Sunday we found a fellow in Providencia reading a Gospel of John which I had given him. I came across a drinking party outside one of the homes, under a shelter. I gave them a message, with several different reactions, I assure you. The best part is that one of them received the Savior, and later gave a grand testimony, indicating that he knew what he had done and was rejoicing in his newly-found Friend!

May 5, 1949—Last Thursday [Bob] Greenman and I scootered to Piquete (45 mi. round trip) to look up a couple of isolated believers, of which we had heard. We were beginning tract distribution, when a kid came running up and said his mother was waiting for us to visit them. He was all excited. We could see the Indian women, standing outside the row of shacks, waving and beckoning to us. This kid had been to the San Antonio Conference, recognized us, and spread the word that the missionaries were there! The story spread like wildfire throughout the village and surrounding Indian camps. The kid's mother and father were Christians, and there were about half a dozen more in their area, we later learned. For years, no one had been there to encourage their hearts. One dear little old woman said, as she cried for joy at the arrival of God's messengers, "We really thought nobody cared for our souls after all." Most can't read, and the only food for them was Easdale's infrequent visits, the last about 4 years before. What a wonderful time we had!

Some youngsters helped us get tracts to every home in the village and nearby settlements. We had a service for the believers during the long noon hour when the men were home from work in cane fields or refinery. They were broken hearted when we said we couldn't stay for a few days, due to meetings back in S. Pedro area. They wouldn't let us go without setting a date for returning; we decided on Tuesday the 3rd. Before we left, the father-in-law of one of the believers, who happened to be visiting from his village, came to Christ. He joyfully agreed to be back to see us Tuesday, and begged us to come to his village.

Tuesday we traveled toward Piquete again, prepared to stay overnight. The scooter motor failed near our destination. Greenman got a ride into Piquete. I limped in with the scooter, just in time for a grand dinner they had prepared for us. We visited during the afternoon and then held an open-air meeting near the shack of some of the believers. A gang of folks gathered, attracted by the bright light of the Coleman pressure lamp, and the blast of my trumpet. The Lord showed His power. We sang for the longest time, had prayer, and Bob spoke. Then more music, and I spoke. Time doesn't mean much here, and we were making up for years of drought from hearing the Word of God. At the open invitation, the first to respond was the wife of the man who received Christ the week before. He couldn't come but had sent his wife and two children from Palmeras. The two children also came to Christ. In total, some

14 professed to receive Christ! What a service! No one wanted to leave afterwards, so we had a sort of after service, sang praises, and listened to the testimonies of several who had been born again that evening! I could go on and on about all the details, indicating the Hand of the Lord with us and blessing at every turn!

The next morning, a young man came to the shack where we had stayed. He explained that he had heard the service from a distance in the dark the night before, and that he wanted to decide for Christ. He did and went on his way rejoicing! We planned a meeting with the believers for noon hour, for final instructions in living and witnessing, before we headed for home. At that meeting, two came in tears. They had heard the night before, and couldn't stand the conviction any longer, and had to come to the Savior. Then three other YP [young people?] accepted the Lord!! The Spirit's working was beautiful! What wonderful answers to prayer!!! This trip alone is worth all it cost to get here and stay here in His harvest field!! We're well, have a girl to help Janet so she can study Spanish, and a Spanish teacher for several days a week! We are bubbling over!

August 1949—Our Blessed Lord knew the value of the individual, Nicodemus, the woman of Samaria, Nathaniel, Andrew, Zacchaeus, and many others. The Lord has led us this month to individuals who needed Him. As we started to one of our meetings, we took a back road instead of the main highway. We wondered why we had decided to go that way but found the Lord was leading. As we passed a shack, miles from any other dwelling, a man rushed out into the road and waved for us to stop. He asked if we were the Gospel messengers, and when we assured him that we were, he asked for a Bible. He had been led to the Lord years ago by the original pioneer of this area now worked by CBFMS. Then he went to Bolivia, joined the Army, lost his Bible, and wandered into sin and disinterest in the things of God. One day, we passed in the truck, and (as we try always to do) tossed out a tract. As he read that wonderful message of God's love, his heart grew warm, and he longed for the joy and peace he had once known. Conviction of sin grew. He longed to get right with the Lord, and get another Bible. He watched constantly for the green truck, from which the leaflet had been thrown. So God led us down that back road until we found the wandering sheep, who confessed his sin and straying and returned to joy and peace in Christ. We will take him a Bible soon!

On another occasion, we had to cancel a street meeting because of a political broadcast, blasted to the whole town by loudspeakers. Disappointed, we went to another settlement, and set up for a meeting. A mere handful came out to listen, and we were praying about what to do next. After the brief service, with no visible results, we began packing up to leave. A fellow, who had stood at some distance on the edge of the woods, came to Jerry and asked how to become a believer. When asked why he wanted to be a Christian, he explained that he had been watching the life of a fellow, Ruben Flores, who was the only believer in the area. After observing him for many months, he said, "I want to be like him." It was so easy to lead that prepared soul to the Savior. Once again we were led by peculiar steps to an individual hungry heart. And about two weeks later, while visiting the new convert, we had the joy of leading his wife to Christ. There's another individual safely in the fold. Reminds us of the **Sunday School** hymn, "Win Them One by One" (If to Christ our only King/Men redeemed we strive to bring/ Just one way this may be done/We must win them one by one)!!'[1]

Mendieta Sugar Co—The first three we baptized on the Mendieta property . . . in Piedritas, probably the smallest village in the company. Our favorite spot was Emilio, across the river from the refinery, and the largest village on the property. Our truck was stoned there a couple of times, and the window broken early on. But after a while, many stories could be told of the power of God in that place! Our continual tract distribution and open-air meetings were used by the Lord in the life of S[eño]r. Dias. His aching, sinful heart cried out for help, and, during a later visit, we introduced him to the Lord. He hurried home ahead of us to tell his family. When we arrived, we watched him lead his wife to Christ, before our eyes, checking the steps with us to see that he was doing it correctly! During the week, three of his children followed.

Then the enemy struck. Dias was an ox-driver. One day the oxen panicked and stampeded. In his attempt to stop them, he fell in the furrows, and part of the plow passed over his body. He ended up in the company hospital. The enemy worked hard during those boring days of convalescence, but the new convert kept his eyes on Jesus. He and his wife, each in his place, was rejoicing in the Lord, in spite of the difficulties. The neighbor family noticed this and soon asked for a Bible. When we sold them the Book, we called their attention to some important verses. Their interest and understanding grew. On a subsequent visit, we saw this tough plantation cowboy kneel on the dirt floor of his humble shack. Amidst the simple improvised furniture, boxes, harness and saddle, and the endless hum of flies, we led him to the foot of the cross. Then his son, who had witnessed his confession of sin and repentance, came out from his hiding place and whispered something in his dad's ear. He wanted to do what his father had done. The father checked, "Could he also, as a lad?" I had no doubt after asking if he was a sinner like his dad, and with tears [he] invited the Lord Jesus into his life. Then the mother appeared from the cooking area out back and also accepted Christ. What joy and thanksgiving filled us! And all because of the testimony of Dias! How can we call that beautiful eternal plan of God an "accident"??

We needed a place for meetings in Emilio, where these families could study the Bible, pray, and worship together. The company would not give us space to build, and there were no vacant buildings in the village. The shacks are small, and meeting in a home had to be abandoned. We had held meetings in the open air, but the rainy season was upon us, and something had to be done. Finally, Dias told us what he had planned while in the hospital. His

---

1. Composed by C. Austin Miles in 1915.

Scenes like this were the greatest desires of the Baptist missionary. Note the different phrases to talk about responding to the gospel. Note, too, the sense that God's providence arranged for such occasions.

Eventually most congregations would build or acquire worship spaces. In the early stages, however, it was common to improvise. The mission society's policy emphasized a self-supporting approach for the new churches. Even when spaces were built or acquired, the aesthetic remained simple.

shack is in two sections in the form of the letter L. He said the place where the two arms join could be covered with a roof, and it would serve for a meeting place! Problem solved! I might add that, due to some kind of technicality, the entire work in La Mendieta was closed to us for about four months in April of 1950. But God answered prayer and His power overruled. The temporary closing was a blessing, for it made the new believers depend on Him and His Word, instead of on the missionary! We were encouraged afterwards to see what the Lord had done!

April 10, 1950—Easter Conference was held here in S[an]. Pedro and was glorious! [The] speaker was Juan Mares, graduate of B[uenos] A[ires] Bible Institute, a fine 21-year-old. He plans to stay on for a while to help here in the north.

The Easter Conference was one of the big yearly worship events. It had a strong emphasis on evangelism. Outside preachers were often scheduled.

La Bajada and Fraile Pintado (truck farming villages)—This story begins up in southeastern Bolivia where Leandro came to Christ. In the late 1940s, he crossed the border into north Argentina and obtained work in a truck farming area near Fraile Pintado (Painted Friar). He was extremely lonesome for there were no Christians there. He prayed that the Lord would let him win someone for a companion, or bring another Christian to his area.

Praying Together—After some time, another believer showed up to work there, and they began reading the Bible and praying together. Friends caught them praying and asked what they were doing. "Talking to God" was their answer. Fellow-workers derided them and frequently reminded them that, since they were not priests, they could not talk to God. Often their praying together at noon hour was interrupted by scoffers and bullies who tried to break up their little meetings. They continued faithful, and soon one of the laborers asked if he could come and listen to them talk to God. Leandro readily agreed, if he would behave and not make fun of them.

A popular pre–Vatican II clericalism that relied upon the clergy to mediate with God is evident in this derision. Developing the ability to pray individually, in small groups, or in larger worship settings was often part of spiritual formation for the new Baptist converts.

Group Growing—Before long, their new visitor asked if he could learn to talk to God like that. Leandro explained that his sin kept him from going into God's presence, and that he must come God's way, through Jesus Christ. When he understood the plan of salvation, he received Christ into his life and took part in the prayer meetings. Others followed, and the group soon was outgrowing Leandro's humble rustic dwelling.

Visit to San Pedro—Along about that time two men appeared at our front door in San Pedro. One was carrying a beat-up gospel tract. He asked if the name stamped on the back was mine, and I assured him it was. I invited them in. One of them was Leandro. They told me the story we have just shared with you. They said the tract was thrown from an army truck. They had followed the address to find us because they needed help and teaching. We prayed with them and promised to help as soon as we could adjust our heavy schedule. Before they left, we loaded them down with literature and simple, printed Bible studies. We also gave them instructions about studying God's Word and recommended verses and chapters for them to consider together. It was sort of a condensed "Bible Institute" training for these two new Christian leaders! Before long, we had another visit from them to tell us that there were several of them ready for baptism!

First Baptisms—We visited them in La Bajada, near Fraile Pintado, where they had built themselves a rustic chapel. After we led a few weekly Bible studies on the subject of baptism, we examined the new believers that were candidates for that biblical ordinance. We found that Leandro had done a remarkable job of sharing the teachings from God's Word, which he had learned in Bolivia. We planned a baptism service and baptized nine. Their brilliant, glowing testimonies thrilled us and impressed others who gathered beside that irrigation ditch. This resulted in others coming to Christ.

Regular Bible studies were an important aspect of Baptist church life, whether for sustaining long-time members, forming new converts, or quickening those who had begun to think about responding to the gospel. The heavy reliance upon the Bible was not only traditional for these Baptists, but it also provided a contrast to Catholicism.

Regular Bible Studies—We continued weekly Bible studies with them, teaching about the local church, Christ the Head of the church, the Lord's Supper, and related truths. The new group prayed and waited on the Lord concerning God's will for leadership and later chose three elders. They began having the Lord's Supper and functioning as a church. They started to reach out to the community. Others came to the Lord. Then they asked if I would baptize 14 more who wanted to become part of the church! They were puzzled when I declined. I proposed another series of Bible studies to explain why I had said "no." They packed the place for these classes, curious to learn what we would show them from the Bible.

More Studies—"The Church"—For several weeks we reviewed the truth that the Church is His; Christ is the Head. The missionary is only His messenger. They (the believers) are God's people in that community. He would lead them and cause them to function for His glory, whether I was present or not! They should depend on Christ, the Head of the Church, to find out who would be His choice to actually do the baptizing. Also, the church should hear the testimony of the candidates and question and examine them. We pointed out that they would always have Him and His Word with them. They might not always have me there!! Meanwhile, I would be available for counsel, and to help them find the part of the Word that applied to decisions and problems, if they needed help. They finally agreed, reluctantly, a date was set and they urged me to be present for the baptism service.

Baptisms in this mission were for those who could speak for themselves and testify to an experience of salvation. Such baptisms were an important window into these Baptists' approach to salvation and the church. The baptisms usually occurred outside in agricultural ditches.

The day arrived. Just before the hour to leave for the service, the truck broke down, and I could not get there. The Lord wonderfully blessed! The candidates gave their testimonies beside the irrigation ditch, some in Guaraní, some in Spanish. One of the leaders was chosen to do the actual baptizing. Another gave a message explaining salvation and baptism, and many of the curious Indians who had come found the Savior!

Spontaneous Expansion—From then on they could not be held back. They had tasted the joy of seeing God work in and through them, and rejoiced together under His leadership. They continued to hold the Lord's Supper and baptismal services, sometimes without even notifying us. We were praising the Lord! They loved that building they had constructed, poles and thatched roof. It was theirs. It was built by their own hands, just because they loved the Lord, wanted to worship Him and proclaim His message. They had to enlarge it from time to time as the numbers attending increased. At one point, they had to fell a tree that was in the way of further growth.

Intentional Wholesome Church Split—One Indian said, "We walk six miles, one way from my home in Maiz Negro ('Black Corn,' across the state highway) to attend meetings here. We do that four times a week. I and others from Maiz Negro are now baptized. Why can't we begin a church in my village and help solve the congestion here?" Good idea! Another group in Fraile Pintado along the state highway made a similar suggestion. They walked three miles each way. Excellent idea! So the whole church agreed to become three churches! We continued to teach and train each of these three groups. We counseled with them and their leaders and continued teaching Bible studies in each congregation.

January 1951—Death is the same everywhere, but the funerals certainly are different! With no embalming here, the law only allows a 24 hour limit between death and burial in this hot climate. This week the 3 year old daughter of a believer in Palo Blanco died, and the father, Ruben, pedaled his bike 8 miles (each way) to tell us in San Pedro. Deeper than the pain of that dark hour was the burden his heart has carried for over 11 years because of his unsaved wife. Only his deep sobbing told the story of hours of tears, as he pleaded with God for the soul of his companion. Now she was making plans for the popular pagan rites with their superstition and drinking through the night in the presence of the remains of the deceased.

With mixed emotions, Ruben explained how much he would like to have us visit the home, but asked us not to go because of the sinful atmosphere which would certainly result from the carousing during the wake. He asked us to meet him at the settlement cemetery, out in the country, the following noon and have a service at the time of burial. After a time of blessed fellowship in the Lord, Ruben started pedaling back that long road which led to the darkness of his village.

A precious time of prayer was held with Dr. Baker, Dr. Cole, and the missionary colleagues before leaving for the funeral. Dr. Baker and I were waiting at the rustic gate of the plantation workers' cemetery, when the huge, two-wheeled cart arrived, drawn by 6 mules. At the gate, the back of the cart was opened and the family and friends climbed down. One big fellow placed the little home-made coffin, with the small body in it, on his shoulders and started down the path between the endless wooden crosses which marked the graves. . . . Friends of the family always help digging and filling the grave. . . . Finally the grave was ready. The top was nailed on the box, and it was handed down to the big fellow in the pit.

It is so easy to think that traditional or cultural matters, from our background, are essential to the Lord's work overseas. To the Argentine, they are "foreign." We unconsciously tend to emphasize whatever was linked with the gospel in our past experience as important, even necessary, when it may be just cultural baggage we are carrying. Paul's method and attitude of knowing nothing among them but Christ, and Him crucified is God's way.

For instance, when the believers in San Antonio said the Sunday morning service was at 6:00 a.m., our hearts cried out that it should be at 11:00 a.m. That is familiar, traditional with us. We tried to correct them, to get them to see the light! They graciously agreed to our schedule. It didn't take long to change it back again, after the first time we tried sitting under that low tin roof following sunup in the tropics the first Sunday!

Had a rough time in Barro Negro last night. We showed Bible story slides midst guffaws and jeers, deliberate noise and name-calling, and finally left town with rocks bouncing off the truck! It was nice of them to wait until we were inside the truck, or they might have been bouncing off our heads! That town is full of Catholics and hoodlums, but they need our Lord, and we are trying to get the message to them. We have inundated that village with literature several times. Pray for Barro Negro ("Black Mud").

January 1953—(Special salute and thanks to three churches for special Holiday gifts.)—Two years ago we sat here and wrote you about the Flores family of the village of Palo Blanco. The 3 year old daughter had just died, and her father, Ruben, notified us to meet them at the cemetery. He warned us not to go to his house, since his hard, unbelieving wife had started the pagan rites with all the drinking, etc. His deep sobs reminded us of the 11 years of heartache since he had found Christ, 11 years of living with a woman who hated the gospel and did all within her powers to make him miserable. Ruben remained true to the Lord and to his wife, but suffered deep pain in his soul. He prayed continually for the salvation of his companion. We ended that prayer letter with these words, "Pray for Ruben as he shines for Jesus in that dark neighborhood of Palo Blanco. Pray for his wife, that her stubborn heart may be melted by the Spirit of God. Pray for those who accompanied that little body to the graveyard, and there heard the message of Eternal Life in Christ Jesus, perhaps for the first time. God answers prayer."

Dr. Baker and Dr. Cole of CBFMS were visiting us at that time and returned to the USA praying and calling on others to pray for Ruben's wife. Many of you received our letter and began to pray for her and for those who heard the gospel at the cemetery. Hundreds, perhaps thousands both here and in the States joined Ruben in interceding for his village and his partner. Then we watched the Hand of God work. One of the men who dug that grave came to Christ a few weeks later, unable to stand the haunting feeling that one day

The Baptist missionaries learn the hard way to think about appropriate cultural adaptation of worship.

someone would dig a grave for him, and he wasn't ready to die. Others found the Savior in Palo Blanco. Ruben was thrilled and grateful to the Lord, but his wife remained hard and cold. Those 11 years of his praying for her, stretched on into the 12th, and then the 13th. Letters from the States came asking, "Has Ruben's wife come to Christ yet?" We had to answer, "Not yet, keep praying!" Jerry talked to her at length on Sunday, the 4th of this month. The sudden death of our milkman, a dear friend of theirs, made a deep impression on her. With this wedge, we dealt with her at length about her soul and her future. We almost hesitated to ask her to make a decision, for we had led up to that dozens of times and had heard her "No!" We hated to give her another chance to reject Him. We prayed, and asked the question. This time the answer was "Wait." We reminded her that she had told the Lord to wait for 13 years and that she should say a decisive yes or no. She promised to do it alone before our next visit, and to tell us when we returned. On the following Sunday, she told us that on Monday, the 5th, she had given her heart to the Savior. God answers prayer!

Source: C. D. Gerow and Janet Gerow, *Letters from Huacalera* (privately published and copyrighted, 1996). These materials are used by permission of the estate of Janet Gerow. No other use or reproduction is allowed without written permission of this estate.

Ronald Olson's Account of His Missionary Activities in the Agricultural Lowlands

The following excerpts are from the unpublished diary of Ronald Olson from 1954, when he and his wife, Darlene, arrived on their mission field, until 1964, when they returned to the United States. As in the Gerow material above, the excerpts were selected to show the nature of this mission's evangelism and worship. The adjoining towns of Ledesma and Libertador, in the agricultural lowlands of northwest Argentina, are prominent.

Like the Gerows, the Olsons, as North Americans, work at navigating the economic and ethnic complexities of the area. Not only does this material make occasional mention of their own interaction with a new culture and peoples, sometimes reflecting their own inevitable ethnocentrism, but it also hints at the social complexities of the area. Note that much of the initial success of the ministry comes from the Bolivian immigrant workers of Amerindian ethnic background.

October 7, 1954, Jujuy Area, First Impressions—I'm much impressed with the multitudes living here in brick and bamboo houses on the sugar plantation and around the factories. Indians galore, sugar cane, hot dusty roads and trails, irrigation ditches and blooming cactuses—all this is northern Argentina. This part of the land seems more like the conventional mission field as pictured in the homeland. By contrast, Salta and Cerrillos seem sparsely settled and more like the USA: normal homes and shopkeepers and farmers, office employees and mechanics—with the only difference being the language and the almost total lack of evangelical witness.

Where God is calling us is yet unknown to us—the north or south, the conventional envisioned missions, or the towns and villages so like those at home. When it's time, the Lord will direct, sustain, and give us a love for the people.

October 11, 1954, Calilegua—We arrived yesterday at Hatcher's (another CBFMS missionary) to visit another part of our field. This is the Florida of Argentina: citrus fruit in abundance, flowers, cane. Tomorrow a conference begins here of around 200 believers. What preparations! We cleaned out 3 metal oil drums to hold water, orange juice, and soup—not too sure how hygienic they are, however.

Calilegua is a "company town" of the Leach Sugar Refinery with the Easdales as administrators, Argentine-born missionary kids of English descent [these Easdales were the children of the Plymouth Brethren missionary Thomas Easdale mentioned above]. The Gospel is freely preached here for that reason. The company owns everything, houses, chapel, etc.

More and more we're thrilled with the work in Calilegua. Last night we visited the windowless shacks (company owned) of the Bolivians who work the harvest. 15 were present inside a bamboo enclosure, topped with a grass roof. A flickering kerosene lantern illuminated and we sat on rough makeshift benches. The method of Bible instruction was simple. Each one read a verse and tried to explain what it meant. Sometimes they needed the words put in their mouths. Then the missionary, Mel Hatcher, would amplify the explanation. We also memorized cards from the Navigators (an American parachurch organization) and Mel gave stars for every verse learned.

January 18, 1955, Placement on Field, Cerrillos—In Cerrillos I have begun going door to door with tracts. So far I've covered over half the main street. I plan to do this monthly, offering a gospel of John, then the John Bible course, hoping eventually to be invited into the homes and to begin a Bible study in a home.

February 14, 1955, Valentine's Day, the First Convert in Cerrillos—Valentine's day and Ofelia found the "lover of her soul," Jesus Christ. What a Valentine's gift to us, too, from Him. Just think, our first "fruit" in Argentina, the girl who works in our home, sees us at our best or worst and wanted Him who makes our home Christian. We knew it was the hour of decision. [What would have happened] had we not given her the last two lessons of the Bible course and attached a decision card, too? And there was a place for a clear decision both on the card and within the lesson itself.

She said "yes" to the invitation in the lesson, but left the card unsigned, because she

---

Note the colonial model: the children of British descent (white) were the administrators, and the Amerindians, the workers. Given the power inequity, could some of the Bolivians have attended out of a desire to please the administration?

While the American-born missionaries held the traditional Baptist idea that people could read the Bible for themselves under the direction of the Holy Spirit, this has been a radical seed emanating in greater democratic political sensibilities. How might widespread literacy and the emphasis upon the individual's authority to interpret the Bible contribute to the rise of democracies?

didn't know what she was supposed to do. Before coming to work that morning she had decided to give her heart to Christ. Darlene had a sweet time of prayer for her and with her.

How heaven rang with angel chorus over her salvation. And how we rejoice after these months of labor to see a soul saved. She is the "firstfruits," the token of many more we are sure that God will give to us.

March 19, 1955, Monday, Cerrillos, the Power of the Simple Word—I am learning something from experience that I have always given lip service to. God blesses His Word. People hunger for His Word. It is amazing; I cannot help but marvel at the drawing power and interest holding power of the Word of God. Last night again (only the 2nd time), we held a Bible study in the home. Beginning with Colossians 1, each one read a verse and afterward simply explaining it, choosing some word from the verse to amplify or illustrate, looking at a parallel passage, [and] asking simple questions. Never have I experienced greater fluency nor grander blessing than in simple fashion attempting to unfold the Word. It works wonders with them. Outlines, sermons, etc., all have their place I am sure, but perhaps I have had too much "sermon," too much "outline" to see the simple yet powerful influence of the bare naked Word of God. It should be no surprise to me to see God use His own Word, either, but it [is].

Reading plays an important role in the story of this Baptist missionary work. The CBFMS missionaries in Argentina benefited from increasing rates of literacy from public education.

April 4, 1955, Cerrillos, Converts—I arrived 1 1/2 hours late in Rosario, and they had begun long ago. I asked, seeing a new face, "Who is this?" It was Hipolito Morales, a nephew of Juan Morales. We had a message, the *cena* (the Lord's Supper), and then sipped *mate*. Rosa de Carrizo left and Juan and Leonard stayed to study sermons. So did Hipolito. When we had a moment free to talk alone, I asked if he was a believer. No, he wasn't a believer, just a listener (an *oyente* or "hearer"). He was a shoemaker, 24 years old. We had been looking up verses and picking out themes for sermons from them, but here was an obviously interested unbeliever right at my side. What a tragedy if Juan and Leonard learned to preach, but Hipolito didn't learn to know the Savior. And so, beginning in John and then in Romans, I picked out salvation verses, but did not only explain how to use them in sermons, but explained the way of salvation from John 1:12; 3:16, 18, 36; 5:24; 10:5 and Romans 1:16; 3:23; 6:23; 10:9–10, 13. And at Rom 10:13 we stopped. "Wouldn't you like to be saved?" I asked Hipolito. He replied, "Yes!" And so we bowed our heads and a son was born, a Savior received, a pardon given. Hipolito, the shoemaker, left the mud adobe home with me on our bicycles, the son, the saved, the saint. Though I was pedaling my bicycle home through the night I was lighthearted for I knew that a new name was written down in glory, where there is no night. Beyond the rare wisps of moonlight peeking through the cloudy sky I seemed to hear the rejoicing in heaven of choirs of angels.

Mate is a popular drink made by steeping dry leaves of yerba mate in hot water.

An important aspect of Baptist piety is utter reliance upon the Bible as the inspired revelation of God. Notice the sequence of verses used in the following entry to lead someone to a decision for Christ. The Word had its own power apart from people.

July 26, 1955, Ledesma, Early Days—This begins our 5th week in Ledesma. We have enjoyed the blessings of the Lord already in the little work we have done. On Saturday night, we had a Bible study again in the book of Colossians. Our attendance has doubled, 11 altogether came, and one very fine prospect from the *ingenio* (a Spanish word for factory or sugar refinery), S[eño]r. Aguilar. Adrian, who brought him, said they talked that night about the Lord until 1 a.m. His wife, too, is interested. I must drop by to visit them this week, second row of houses, number 27.

Sunday we had the *cena* (the Lord's Supper) and afterward decided without a dissenting voice to buy individual communion cups instead of use one cup for everyone. Then we had our first study on the doctrine of the church with an attendance of 17.

How might the adoption of individual cups have been perceived by the locals who were used to sharing *mate* by sipping from the same straw? Could the absence of dissent have been as much a matter of respect for the missionaries as a consensus about standards for hygiene?

August 8, 1955, Ledesma—The day began with both of us a bit sick and ended with both of us really exhausted, but not any sicker. Only 11 came to communion; it seemed all the men choose to be absent the same day. Nonetheless, it was a good meeting, and for the first time we used individual communion cups.

I invited Arturo to eat with us and go to San Antonio afterward to distribute tracts. Our meal was interrupted by three men: one from Maiz Negro, a second man from Santa Rosa, and a third from Elena. The fellow from Elena had come to arrange a meeting on his *lote* and after finding out how to get there (11 kilometers) we decided on next Sunday afternoon. After this Arturo and I walked to San Antonio up toward the mountain and distributed *La Voz* (a publication meaning The Voice) and met the believer living there. We rested in his home, talked and prayed and returned by the main street distributing more tracts.

We had coffee and Darlene left for Sunday School and I followed in an hour with our two children in the wagon. Some of the men had returned by then, and there were two unsaved men at the meeting. The Lord gave real freedom and blessing in preaching on Christ, the Light. I have real hope for Carlos Bustamante and feel he is the key to his mother's conversion, Lidia.

Conducting worship in Spanish was only a partial step toward full inculturation of Baptist worship for these Amerindian converts, since Spanish was brought to them by colonizers. Spanish was better than the Latin of the Catholic Mass, but it was still not their first language home.

August 15, 1955, Ledesma—Yesterday was some day! But let's go back to the day before. No sooner had we got in the house than a young fellow came to the door, greeted me with a hug (two of them!), and called me "My pastor." He wanted baptism, but I'd never seen him before in my life. He left returning moments later with Doña Saturnina. He hardly talked Spanish, but she was sure he ought to be baptized.

That evening I brought the matter up in our Bible study, asking the rest. Although he was unknown (due to the circumstances of his work which caused him to continually move), after hearing his testimony, the brethren thought it was all right.

It was a chilly Sunday morning when we arrived at the irrigation canal. The water was even chillier. The fellow removed his trousers, revealing long underwear. I hid a smile. After prayer and a hymn we entered the icy water where I baptized him, baptizing myself, too, since I slipped on the bottom when I brought him up. At the *cena*, we had more participants than cups ready since 14 took the *cena*.

At 1 p.m., Mateo, Arturo, and I left for *lote* Elena by bicycle, 11 kilometers into the heart of the sugar refinery (*ingenio*). It was good to spend a short time with a few believers there and to make plans to return in September. We left literature, and Arturo and Mateo spoke. The village was really hidden away, the homes of logs and mud with tin roofs, fences of cane. Tired, hot, thirsty, we got back just in time for Darlene to leave for Sunday School. None of her children came on time.

At the p.m. service we were about 25, hardly enough seats for all of us. Two unsaved adults were present, Carlos and Juana, plus several children that hadn't come previously. It was an exhausting day with 5 meetings, but a happy tiredness in the service of the Lord. I felt the blessing and inner pleasure of the Lord throughout the day.

> What it means to be "on time" is very culturally influenced. Would American cultural sensitivities have been different from those of their parishioners in this matter?

September 20, 1955, Perón Falls—What all this means for us is uncertain. We can only trust the Lord who brought us here to preserve and keep us. The power of the Catholic Church is vastly increased with the going of Perón. Whether they will take advantage of their privilege to persecute the Evangelicals is to be seen.

October 12, 1955, Ledesma—At 3 o'clock, Ron went to the *local* (church meeting place) and started the windup Victrola with Gospel recordings, and the folks began to come. After greeting one another, we began singing choruses, "Isn't He Wonderful?" (It's recorded in God's Word./Isn't Jesus, my Lord, wonderful?),[2] "Only Believe," etc. We had some testimonies, and then Mrs. Aguilar gave hers and asked also for baptism. She is a little Bolivian Indian woman, even shorter than Darlene. The church decided she should be baptized and so the children piled into the Olsons' "new" Model A Ford station wagon (a gift made possible by the generosity of the CBFMS ladies association of Wyoming and Montana). The others started out on foot for the nearest irrigation ditch running alongside the cemetery. (What better place to "die in Christ"?) Then in the muddy waters of the stream, we read how Jesus was baptized in the Jordan river and "buried" (see Romans 6) Mrs. Aguilar in the waters of baptism. When she changed clothes in a dressing room formed of bed sheets held around her by the other women we sang songs of faith.

> The last two lines of the chorus of "Isn't He Wonderful?"— quoted here—underscore two Baptist values: the importance of Scripture and a more affective experience of God. This is one reason the song would be popular among Baptists.

On our return to our orange crate and tree branch church building, the victorious notes of "Up From the Grave He Arose" came from the Victrola. The *mate* was ready to drink when we got back and the women served us. There were 45 people overflowing into all parts of the little house and out into the lot.

2. This chorus was found in multiple songbooks from the mid-twentieth century, sometimes attributed to S. Jones, sometimes to F. H. Carlson, and sometimes to an anonymous songwriter.

October 21, 1955, Ledesma—Today I had my first wedding for a couple with two children already who have lived together for 7 years. They were saved in Cordoba, and [they] want to follow the Lord in Baptism, but the church requires marriage first. Well, better late than never, but it seems a strange first Argentine wedding ceremony for me.

We arrived at the mud and cane houses, one long building with lots of rooms and a separate kitchen shack for each of the families. They hauled out the chair of honor for me, made of wicker or reeds, and a roughhewn table. The rest of the group sat on rough homemade benches with tree branches pegged into them as legs.

The church bell was a long piece of railroad rail struck with a rod of iron. The mothers sat about nursing their infants and [children] up to 1 and 2 years of age. The leader spoke very little Spanish, and none of them appeared to know much of it. I was glad for my helper Mateo Padilla, who speaks Guaraní and explained what I preached to them.

November 19, 1955, Ledesma—Señora Acuña, daughter of our next door neighbor, came in with her two daughters to hear the choruses she had sung as a child when another missionary lived here in Ledesma in the 30's. We have a row house and tin roof, and we share a common wall with the Acuñas. We looked high and wide for the words to "Wide, wide as the Ocean" for her. She was a contrast to the other Bolivian peasants and Indians who one by one entered our home while she was present. Oh, if we could only win her and those like her who in their childhood heard the Word and had it planted in their hearts. Lord, help us begin a Bible study for the upper class people here who have interest in the Bible.

November 25, 1955, Lote Enrique—"Is there anyone here tonight who wants to surrender to Christ?" I asked. "Stand to your feet and tell us." An 18-year-old lad, Rogelio Rios, stood up and hesitatingly said he wanted to be saved. Afterward he was greeted by each of the believers in that quadrangle of mud houses. Two lanterns dispelled the shadows from the dark faces of the Guaraní Indians seated in a circle in the open space between the "longhouses." Rogelio cannot read!

December 10, 1955, Ledesma—"Have you read the New Testament I gave you?" I asked. Luis replied, "Yes, only a few pages to go." "And if you should die tonight, where will you go?" was my next question. I was shocked when he replied with assurance: "To heaven!" But he didn't know why he would go to heaven. It was so simple to lead him from these replies to the Savior and, without a moment's hesitation, he got down on his knees and, in his own words, asked to be saved. So sweet! So sudden! So sincere! Yes, the Word bore fruit. And so did a helping hand. This is the young lad with a flat tire on a rainy night that I stopped to help. I'd get wet again if it meant another soul for Christ!

Olson means strange in the sense that both persons were Argentine and not the Bolivian immigrants with whom he normally ministered.

Why might a minister desire to extend ministry to richer economic classes?

An invitation for personal decision was given at the end of a service, this time with a positive response. The community literally enfolded those who were willing to respond to Christ.

December 31, 1955—Christmas has come and gone, and New Year's is at hand. Christmas Eve we all went to Bananal with Hatchers for a program and baptism. Then Christmas Day we had our program here in our house with 30 altogether. A threatening thunderstorm kept many away, but 30 was a houseful. We showed slides; the children recited their pieces. We then drank lemonade and ate cookies.

I haven't had a chance to talk to Luis Castro since the day he gave his heart to Christ, but Julio Ortiz has shown real spiritual growth since September 17 when he accepted Christ and seemed so wobbly in his first steps of the new life.

January 10, 1956, Lote Enrique—Everyone was glad to see us, their brown faces keen with joy. The record player brought them some Spanish and Guaraní music and sermonettes. I played one about a new heart and another about the Prodigal Son (see Luke 15). Then I gave a brief salvation message with the flannel graph object lesson on the "Bells" and their "Tongues."

At the close, when the invitation was given, a youth, age 19, Vacilio Segundo, gave his heart to Christ. He stepped from the shadows, and there in front of the circle of believers he confessed to being a sinner and asked Christ to forgive him and save him. Afterward, each one shook hands, offered him a word of advice, and welcomed him into the family of the children of God.

February 9, 1956, Clara Royan Accepts Christ—Last night in the rain a young girl stopped me to tell me she wanted to be baptized. I asked when she had accepted Christ, and she said she hadn't. She apparently was confusing baptism and salvation. So this afternoon I went to her home where I could explain how to be saved without standing outside in the rain. She very sweetly and simply asked God to forgive her and save her for Jesus' sake and without emotion showing, gave her heart to Him. I counseled her to wait awhile for baptism and started her in the John Bible course for new converts. She comes from a Christian home, and I trust she will show indication of real new birth.

Julio seems to be in a dry spell, spiritually, lacking the earnestness first manifested. I can only continue to pray for his continued growth and a revival in his heart.

The gas station attendant has been reading the Gospel of John and when I bought gas yesterday, he asked for a Bible. I sold him one and gave him the first lesson of the John course. Another Bible was presented to S[eño]r. Mareco, the *lotero* (the Spanish word for a boss, e.g., the manager of a sugar refinery) of Lote Enrique. He told me that 20 years ago someone had given him one. I hope this time the Bible will get into his heart and life.

Last night in Enrique a lost sheep returned to the fold, but another has gone astray. Jesus Demacio has confessed his sin and returned to the Lord, but Vacilio is out drinking with the boys.

A variety of media was used to present the gospel to worshipers and prospective converts. Notice the multiple languages used.

Notice in this description where different cultural traditions are shared through music and different styles of teaching. In what ways do you think cultural differences make ministry and church life more difficult, especially in situations like these? How often and in what ways does the New Testament address such differences?

March 21, 1956, Ledesma, Salvation of Pascual De Acuña—This morning Pascual stopped by to ask about dedicating his baby to the Lord. I suggested that first he get married and that his wife become a Christian.

Well, this afternoon I thought how nice it would be to take a picture of the new babies, including that of the Aguilares, so [I] dropped by to tell them that tomorrow I'd be by to take their pictures. Then, too, what better way to win the friendship of Pascual's wife and her confidence so that I might tell her of Christ. But it wasn't necessary for she was ready. After a brief talk about having a Christian home and raising the baby to know Christ and to be a son of whom she could be proud, she wanted to be saved.

It was so easy. She didn't know how to pray so I put the words in her mouth for her. Her husband cried with joy over her salvation, and he prayed, too, giving thanks to God.

Easter Conference 1956—Sixty persons jammed like sardines crowded into our home last night which was Good Friday!

The slow chant of many voices was approaching as we were finishing our "chorus time," and I was about to crawl over and through the crowd of people in our living room to get back to the projector and show slides of the Easter story. The chanting crescendo went to a roar as the large Roman Catholic procession neared our house. It was either drown them out or be drowned out. And so as the candles and shoulderborn images slowly passed our home, sixty voices rang out, "Only the Power of God Can Change Your Soul" (Only the power of God can change your soul./The proof I give to you: He has changed me./Don't you see that I'm happy following the Lord?/I'm a new creature. I'm new!)[3] and the words of the chorus "Isn't He Wonderful?" (It's recorded in God's Word./Isn't Jesus, my Lord, wonderful?). The slides and music went well together. There was real reverence in spite of the crowded condition and the many children and babies present.

At the close I gave an invitation to accept Jesus Christ and one lad made his first public testimony and three others were saved: Benita de Rojas, Santiago Rojas and Pedro Carrizo.

As I was explaining afterward to these three how to be saved, Darlene was outside on the sidewalk, answering three high school girls (Argentines who were blondes) asking "What is the difference between you and us?" One of the girls responded to Darlene: "There isn't any difference except that we have a church [building] and they don't." Darlene explained that there was a bit more of difference than that.

May 6, 1956, Ledesma—My Lord called two more to salvation last night, a teenage girl, who after great struggle of soul, stood up to give her heart to Christ. Her name is Concepción Royan. The other 18-year-old lad was a complete stranger to me. His name is Victor

Normally Baptists (among many Christians) would think that prayer needs to arise spontaneously to be sincere. When can a prayer provided by another be authentic?

The tension between the two churches and their ways of worship is exemplified in this episode. The Catholics would have been participating in their traditional Holy Week processions. The Baptists counter with testimonial songs having a strong emphasis upon Jesus Christ.

Darlene Olson identifies the ethnic origin of the teenage girls (they are Argentine, not Bolivian Amerindian) through their hair color.

3. "Solo el Poder de Dios" is the Spanish title. It is possibly a song by Argentine Baptist Roque Barroso. English translation provided by Darlene Olson.

Velazquez. The best I knew how I told him how to be saved. I hesitate to tell anyone to wait to accept Christ until they understand it all. Yet it seems doubtful if some of them know all that being a Christian implies but, then, who of us knew when we received Christ all that it meant.

This morning was a red letter time, too. Four obedient children of God were baptized in the way their Savior was. They were:

- Felipe Calancha
- His wife
- Benita de Rojas
- Santiago Rojas, her father

Yes, at long last Felipe and his wife have won the battle to be married and baptized! How happy I was to be witness at the civil ceremony at the city hall last Friday night. How I praise the Lord to have Felipe as a member in full standing of our local church. I trust God will keep him here to serve Him and to help build God's work in this town.

May 12, 1956, Luchan—The first time I ever went to the cane village of Luchan was on February 2. Then a young drunk entered the meeting when it was half over and happily drunk, loudly proclaimed that he wanted to become a Christian. I wasn't too sympathetic and told him to return again when he was sober and could understand the message.

Upon arrival there was nothing new to encourage me: the same halfhearted believers, the same listeners whom each week I had begged to accept Christ.

But this young fellow from that first meeting, then so drunk, listened. He laughed with his friend, with me or at me, I wasn't sure. But, when the simple invitation was given, he said he wanted to be saved. It certainly seems to be God's answer to whether it is worth it to go there. Furthermore a woman came for the first time who wants to return to Christ once more. She is saved and baptized, but married to an unbeliever who is very hardhearted.

July 10, 1956, Ledesma, First Weekend Evangelistic Conference—We had three precious blessed days of special meetings here in Ledesma with Roque Barroso as our speaker. July 9 is Independence Day in Argentina, and, since it fell on a Monday, we had a real long weekend. His messages met a real need and were varied.

- A message on false doctrines.
- Communion[;] he spoke on Mary and Martha and choosing the better part.
- A salvation message on the unhappiness that sin causes.
- A salvation message.

- A message on the Christian home and the importance of training our children in the ways of God.
- A message on Lazarus' Resurrection and our need to "roll away the stone" that Jesus may save the lost.

Altogether 11 professions of faith were made: 9 of them children and 2 youth. The last night our servant girl came and gave her heart to Christ. Then after Sunday School, 7 of our little Sunday School children finally gave in to Jesus. We asked those who wanted to be saved to remain afterward when the rest go home.

November 6, 1956, La Bajada—A long uphill climb on a gravel road lined with willows, the sound of a hurrying irrigation ditch beneath the willows, tomato plants and sugar cane on the horizon as well as lemon trees with thatched huts dropped beneath them. Then the owner's "mansion" surrounded with trucks and wagons. Fruit flies, dark sweaty men and boys, unshaved truck drivers and an occasional horseman in baggy gaucho trousers and a black cowboy felt hat. All this entered my senses on the way to La Bajada near Fraile. The car broke down, and we hiked the rest of the way into the village.

The baptism was a blessing even though not anything special. A small irrigation ditch was dammed by a large piece of sheet metal and reinforced with clods of dirt and sod, making a lovely muddy dark pool about knee deep. The two candidates for baptism were very sincere in this step, and I'm sure it meant a great deal to them. The woman wept as she gave her testimony of faith in Jesus Christ.

1957 Easter Comments—Our first real Easter Conference ended yesterday evening. Three full days, some 24 meetings altogether, and I don't know how many meals were served. [The] Hatchers, Greenmans, and Easdales were a blessed help, and Ernesto Paniagua and his quartet made a big spiritual impact on the folks. It is difficult to assess spiritual results of the conference, but we felt His Spirit at work in the messages. We had special women's meetings and a men's workshop on soul winning. Three boys and girls came to the Lord, also, in the children's meetings of nearly 60 children of all ages in one big class. Five were baptized from here and from Maiz Negro. How we praise the Lord for them and their example to others that are not yet baptized.

May 26, 1957, Ledesma, Leader Dedication—After a brief song service I brought a message of dedication. After the part of the message especially directed to the elders, they knelt at the front bench while two members of the congregation prayed that the Holy Spirit would fill them for this special ministry. Following this, I continued with the part of the message for deacons, and they likewise knelt to receive the prayers of the congregation. Then I addressed some words to the congregation followed by the reading of the church covenant, and, again all standing, we asked the Lord to help us keep the spirit and ideal of the covenant. The message ended with some exhortations for the unbaptized and the unsaved. We felt the meeting was blessed of the Lord and the presence of the Holy Spirit and that the officers left with a sense of their great responsibility.

July 27, 1957, Ledesma—Tonight was a happy meeting at the little church with a nice spirit of love among us. After the meeting several fellows were practicing choruses. I suggested they sing tomorrow night—and I do believe it is the start of a men's chorus. I'm a far cry from a choir director, but I praise the Lord for a very little knowledge of music.

Ledesma's musical ministry takes a step forward with the formation of a men's chorus. A variety of smaller and larger groups would participate in worship.

September 30, 1957, Ledesma—Two were baptized: Jorge Coultard and Olegario Cardozo. It was in the swift flowing irrigation stream. Just before [we entered] into the water, a whiskey bottle floated down stream, perhaps a token of a former life of sin, now washed in the blood [of Jesus Christ].

[Jerry] Gerow spoke before the communion service, after which we had an ***asado*** with all the believers. Most of them remained all afternoon (more or less 50 of them). In the evening, we rented a truck and all went to Calilegua to the tent meetings, a real treat, with around 500 attending: music, slides, a good message. All returned home rejoicing, and we hope with a deeper joyful experience of Christ in their hearts.

An *asado* is an Argentine version of a barbecue.

October 24, 1957, Deacon Trouble—We are having deacon trouble, and just after writing in our last prayer letter of our fine deacons and elders:

- One elder is an adulterer and wishes to leave his wife.
- Another may move and shows no push or drive to help with the Lord's work.
- A third upon whom all the work has fallen has a wife that hinders and is in danger of becoming spiritually proud.
- A fourth has moved away.
- A fifth is rebellious and a church tramp.
- A sixth carries on the work, but his children are becoming a problem to him and his wife.

Also the number of conversions lately is nil, and we seem to be in a dry period. Some people in other places have been saved, but no one in our town for over a month. Well, not quite! A man was saved on September 28 by the name of Maximilliano Vallegas.

Honesty, openness, and specificity were frequent qualities in the way people confessed during worship.

November 1, 1957, Ledesma—Sunday night Pedro, the elder in adultery, confessed his sin and asked for prayer and forgiveness. It changed the whole atmosphere of the church, and after the service Mrs. Zambrano, her daughter, and another were saved. God works.

April 15, 1958, Ledesma—We planned 3 days of precious fellowship for believers in this area. It was all of that! But it was more: a four night evangelistic campaign with souls saved every night, about 25 adults and just as many children in the twice daily children's meetings with Marjorie Hurlbut. Good Friday I estimate 500 listened to the message, people standing 5–6 deep all around the edge of the tent.

October 14, 1960, Libertador—We held a street meeting in Lote Paulina last night for the first time. About 200 harvesters listened, for the most part, quietly, earnestly. We had testimonies, song, [and] special [musical] numbers. Orillio preached very well. The dark and dirty upturned faces reminded me of the multitudes [who] Christ said were sheep without a shepherd. In Lote Paulina we saw men and women like ants, carrying tree trunks, beds, and what have you, as they are moved from one place to another. They appear to have never taken a bath. A little, un-sanded white-washed coffin of a baby, a few flowers on top, was being carried among the other household equipment and firewood. How would Christ have looked at them? Would He have cried out, "Come unto Me, all ye that labor and are heavy laden, and I will give you rest"? (See Matthew 11:28.) Give me, O Savior, Thy eyes, Thy heart, and Thy voice!!!

November 17, 1960, Libertador—Another harvest of souls has come to us with the arrival of Joel Romero, not that it began with him, but it gained momentum. In Prediliana, a lad I'd talked to a couple of times came through under Joel's persuasion at the street meeting. On Saturday five more were saved, three fellows and two girls. Sunday night still another made profession of faith though I was not here in Ledesma. Then at the Christmas practice Tuesday night Manuel Mendoza brought a 20-year-old friend who wanted to be saved, and I led him to Christ while up at the front of the church they continued their play practice for the Christmas program.

January 28, 1962—At the close of the elections the newly elected officers came to the platform and the entire congregation gathered in a circle around them at the front of the church where we sang together, "Take My Life and Let It Be Consecrated, Lord, to Thee." Then they knelt on the platform, and I led in a dedicatory prayer for us all.

February 11, 1962—The church building in Ledesma continues. The form of the front gable is finished, at least the brick work is. It only lacks plastering, and the little round window and the open Bible in marble on the front now. The floor is not laid yet. I've given up on getting the front doors and windows from Vacafloor. On Wednesday the church is to open a checking account, so their financial status will be independent of ours or the missions. It is their own money and they should take care of it themselves now. As a matter of fact, they've pretty well done that with a little help from us, since the beginning. A couple of times our "treasurers" have "borrowed" the Lord's funds for emergency personal need, but they have always returned the funds, eventually!!!

Just returned from Lote Luchan, 25 kilometers or so from here. On the way I did something I seldom do. I picked up 3 lads thumbing their way to Luchan. It didn't just happen that they were boys interested in the gospel. It was God again. The man I went to see in Luchan wasn't home, but these youths came into the house, and I played some disks, "The Two Roads" and "The Rich Man and Lazarus," for them. Then I asked them if they'd like to be saved. Four of them (another had joined us) indicated their desire to be saved. In another adjacent room, we knelt to pray. Some of them seemed very sincere. One of them laughed, whether from nerves or not, I don't know. I have learned long ago not to try to determine which ones are really saved and which are just reciting another evangelical "rosary" for me, to gain merit with whatever powers there be. Their names are Ignacio Solencio, Francisco Vasquez, Valerio Chevelier and Miguel Angel Segundo. All of them are teenagers. Keep them, O Lord, in that wicked village, from the vile scum of sin and give them victory. Amen.

February 21, 1962, Ledesma—Pedro Justo Rodriguez, age 12, Gevaro Cardozo Velasquez, age 25, and Francisco Pancho Andrada, age 27. The latter two are keen lads that have possibilities to be preachers if they follow on. The accent is on youth in the past few months. The Lord has given us 20–25 young people in Ledesma. Our first youth meeting was held last Friday, February 16. Our "new frontier" is the challenge of these young folk. They are full of life and want to be doing. It is great just to be with them—why I even feel younger, stimulated by their vigor and enthusiasm to serve the Lord. They are intelligent and drink in the Word of God, [and] are eager to be taught—what a teaching ministry! They put new blood into the church services. One Sunday night a month the young people will take charge of the evening evangelistic service. They are also beginning a youth chorus. Tonight three of them can't wait to give their testimonies in the village of Maiz Negro (Black Corn), where I am returning after at least 6 months of absence.

February 23, 1962, Ledesma—Tonight, which is chilly and threatening rain, the young people are coming to our house for their first ever choir or chorus practice. Darlene has never tried anything like it, but then no one knows more music here than she does. She plans to teach just two part harmony. Poor girl—not feeling too well either. Hot weather seems to upset her liver with accompanying dizziness and headache—nothing serious enough to tell a doctor, but miserable enough to put up with.

Well, we had 13 show up to practice on our screened-in porch, and it looks real hopeful. Darlene did excellently. It isn't her nature to be dogmatic and firm . . . [she] assigned them their parts and, as a choir director, will "pass muster." The kids seemed to enjoy it, although some of them don't hear too well to sing a second part, [and] so there was plenty of disharmony along with the harmony.

Note the subtle reference to different cultures. One wonders what cultural expectations and desires the fourteen young singers brought to the rehearsal.

March 13, 1962, Ledesma—Fourteen young people met on the back porch for choir practice last night. To "stateside eyes" such a comment means little, but in Ledesma it means that young people who have never sung before, who cannot read music even, who don't discern the difference between tenor and bass, by painstaking practice and great enthusiasm are learning to glorify God in song!!

When I arrived home from Fraile Pintado, the tenors were in the study, the sopranos in the living room, and the altos on the back porch. Sounded like the practice rooms of lower chapel at Wheaton College! [Editor's note: Ronald Olson had attended Wheaton College in Illinois.]

In Fraile Pintado, I spoke last night on the Lord's guidance from the text of Jeremiah 33:3, following some of the thoughts on the pages previous to this. In my mind I was debating whether to cut short the service to visit the brethren up the road in a *quinta* (a small farm) of tomatoes. I hadn't much desire to go and said to myself, "Oh, that it might rain so that we can't go."

Well, rain it did—and blew a strong wind. In blew a young man in the middle of the message. I thought he might be drunk, but it was a case of being breathless, running for refuge in the rain. He had worked for Lobo, the foreman. So instead of rushing off to another meeting, I had the joy of leading him and also a daughter of Mrs. Lobo to the Lord. If it had not rained, I'd have rushed off and if it had not rained, the young man would not have been "blown" into our meeting at all. All of which serves to illustrate the providential circumstances sent of God to guide His children. The man's name is Francisco Fernandez; the lady's name is Mildonia Nelida Perez. Her home is in Urundel. Both persons, though I have never before seen them, had been prepared in heart beforehand. He had gone to Sunday School as a child, and she attended services in Urundel. There was no opportunity for a quiet private conversation with them. They accepted the Lord in the presence of all the others assembled in the room, getting down on their knees on the concrete floor and praying the sinner's prayer with me helping them to express themselves in this unaccustomed conversation with a heavenly Father they'd never spoken to before.

Notice again the pastoral necessity to forgo truly extemporaneous prayer when those wanting to pray have not been formed in the capacity to do so.

April 29, 1962, Ledesma, Sixth Annual Easter Conference—The theme of the conference was the question of the angels at the tomb: "Why seek ye the living among the dead?" (Luke 24:5), a fitting theme in a country given to prayers to the dead saints. The messages in the daytime were of real benefit to the Christians, and in the evening the Gospel was clearly proclaimed by Joel Romero. The colored slides and the gospel band from Coronel Cornejo attracted much attention from the town people, too, and we must have had 500 people in the evening meetings each night.

May 28, 1962, Ledesma—For three days we have been out of this world, at the Baptist Men's Retreat, as it is called. [We had] no radio, no newspaper, no contact with civilization—out in the woods. I slept in my car, parked 2 yards from a gurgling river, in fact, two gurgling rivers. Two big tents of the mission served as a "cathedral" and dormitories for 275 men who registered. The main speaker spoke much to my own heart, especially on the enemies and trials of Joseph (Genesis 37 and following) and the "sleep" of Lazarus (John 11), which he spiritualized as the sins of believers, and the apparent silence and delay of God in delivering us from them. I can't put on paper what happened in my heart, but it was warmed, warned, comforted, and shamed.

Being in charge of the physical elements took away some of the enjoyment: crises in the kitchen, shortages of food stuffs, and all the details of managing a camp, where everything must be brought in and cared for from the outside. However, I feel the camp was a success, and we ended in the black financially.

October 9, 1962, Ledesma—Last Saturday and Sunday nights I did that which I said I would not and could not do: preach in Spanish in a tent in an evangelistic campaign. It was in Palpala, a mining town near Jujuy. I preached two evangelistic sermons to a well-filled tent each night. The Lord did bless, mostly my own heart, in doing this. But also some souls came to the Savior. What I thought I could not do, I did. I don't think my gift is evangelism, and my Spanish is not fluent or good enough to be in the public eye, but I know now that, when we submit to the Lord, He can do and will do anything to give us success.

April 10, 1963, Ledesma, Seventh Annual Easter Conference—"Yo sé que mi Redentor vive" ("I know that my Redeemer lives") is the theme from Job 19:25 of this Easter Conference, now a day away. Preparations are in full swing, including last minutes ones.

Yesterday morning two priests came to our door, didn't knock, but slipped a letter under the door and hurried away. The letter was a strong protest that we were greatly offending the Roman Catholics by having a big barbecue on Good Friday and inviting the entire town.

We wrote a very polite reply saying it was neither a barbecue, nor for the public and quoted Romans 14:5 from the Catholic Bible. The local priest, Msgr. Martinex, a Spanish

Here is another conflict between the Baptists and Catholics over varying practices during Holy Week and Easter.

national, received us very courteously and was very jovial, chuckling to himself as he read our letter, especially the Apostle Paul's words to the church in Rome. He appeared satisfied with our explanation and our wish not to offend the Catholics' tender consciences.

Easter 1963, Ledesma—Our Seventh Annual Easter Conference in Ledesma lasted 3 days and 4 nights, and left us, as always, exhausted. Some 63 decisions were made this year, some real, others perhaps shallow. Six made reconciliation.

There were easily that many backsliders present. The speaker was Pablo Esteve, 28 years old, a Plymouth Brethren, Spanish by birth, whose heart and mind were subject to the Spirit's power. He was a "dark horse" as I'd never heard him speak to sinners. His manner with believers is not dynamic, nor striking, and he is not a "personality." But he had power, God's Power, and more than twice as many were touched as the previous year, not to mention the many who showed no visible manifestation.

One Spanish lady of culture wept for two nights straight during the messages and music. The third night she was converted. A man we've waited for during 5 years came with his broken back in plaster cast, and, at last, gave in to Christ. A young couple in the factory town across the tracks, with whom we've dealt for two months as well as by various friends and relatives, was saved. Several old men, pensioned and retired, were saved. Ten children gave their hearts to Christ.

During the day messages were given by Charles and Jo Green. Their puppet shows were terrific. His messages were well prepared, challenging, emotionally as well as mentally moving. Beverly Jones gave a fine message on Genesis 3. Roque Barroso spoke four times, twice in the tent, and at two street meetings. Other missionaries present who served in various ways were Walter Hoops, Mel Hatcher, Ken Cook and Bob Greenman.

Notice again the racial dynamics at play in this ministry: the office worker at the sugarcane plant was white while the majority of the workers were natives or Bolivian immigrants.

May 15, 1963, Ledesma—Later I visited a young office worker and his wife in the *ingenio* (factory town) in their home, two more hungry souls with white faces, in contrast to the Indian ones in Paulina. They had both listened to the Word preached by us at the street meetings in the *ingenio*. He had bought two Bibles as he had ripped up the former Bible he owned at the command of the Roman Catholic priest. But now, two years later, the seed sown back then is bringing forth fruit. The very book he ripped apart has conquered his soul. Praise God!

August 14, 1963, Tartagal—I am in Tartagal, teaching Joshua to a group of 30 Guaraní Indians, living with the Greens, while Darlene is in Pichanal, holding the fort, I hope, against the Pentecostals! I miss her, as I always do, "with whom I do not have to measure words."

October 17, 1963, Ledesma—We have three Methodists in our home to make a survey of the area with a view to beginning a medical teaching ministry. I have mixed feelings as to their coming and beginning a work near us. But we have given them a cordial welcome, keeping them in our home, and last night they spoke in the Ledesma church.

Well, the Methodists are gone, and I am tired. The nervous strain is what exhausts. We didn't expect them to stay so long. They wanted to see "the Indian settlements" of our area. We don't have any, strictly speaking. They want an Indian work to do.

November 14, 1963, Pichanal—Monday through Wednesday nights were spent in Santa Rosa. Oh, where are the pastors of the flock? I guess one has turned Pentecostal. The pastor we had in Santa Rosa is still pastoring the flock, but not our flock. It is still God's flock, however. I find myself in the unwelcome or unhappy position of polemicist defending the Baptist position. I like the trowel better than the sword, at least when it comes to doctrinal error among simple folk who do not reason well. I preached 2 Tim. 1:13 last night in our little chapel: "Hold fast the form of sound words which thou hast heard of me in faith and love which is in Christ Jesus."

Our meeting ended at 8:30 p.m., and the Pentecostals began with a young woman preaching at the meeting just 25 feet away. I went to talk with Felipe and Solema to be friendly and also to discuss having the meeting at the same hour as their[s] because of their raucous singing and clapping disturbing ours.

The Catholics were not the only ones who could trouble the Baptists. The more ecstatic worship of the Pentecostals seemed intentionally placed in this instance to highlight the conflict.

January 6, 1964, Ledesma—We attended the Plymouth Brethren communion service on Sunday a.m. It was so stiff and formal, the hymns so slow, [that] I thought I was in the Lutheran Church again. There are long periods of silence while waiting for the Holy Spirit to lead.

Ronald Olson had grown up Lutheran.

March 13, 1964, Ledesma—This is our fifth night of meetings for Christians in the Ledesma Church. It is the last night of "the deeper life" conference in preparation for Easter week. Charles Green has spoken of the following themes:

1. El Cuerpo Formándose [the body (the church) being formed]
2. El Cuerpo Relacionándose [the body in relationship]
3. El Cuerpo Trabajando [the body working]
4. El Cuerpo Sanándose [the body being healed]
5. El Cuerpo Aumentándose [the body growing itself]

1 Corinthians was the basis for all the messages. Attendance has been good, and although no invitations have been given, nor have we seen any attempt for an emotional spiritual crisis, yet there has been, we believe, a deepening of heart understanding that will make a difference in lives and relationships between members of the body.

March 23, 1964, Ledesma—The first meeting of the Easter campaign began last night with a packed-out tent and many people standing outside. Everything went off smoothly because of the hard work of everyone beforehand. Walter Hoops and a team of men took care of the children in the church building for special children's classes.

The whole town has been covered with invitations and special *avisos* [announcements] and the network of loudspeakers around town announce every hour along with strains of "The Old Rugged Cross" playing.

The Olsons left Argentina in the summer of 1964 and worked for the next several years in the United States. Eventually they returned to the mission field.

March 30, 1964, Ledesma—The Eighth Annual Easter Conference ended last night after 8 days of meetings for adults and children. Twenty-three persons professed faith in Christ. Three were reconciled to Him. We had good weather and the tent was packed with many standing outside each night.

Source: Used by permission of the Olson family.

Jerry and Janet Gerow Begin a New Phase of the Baptist Missionary Work

In late 1954, just as the Olsons were arriving on the field, the Gerows began a new venture in the CBFMS efforts in northwest Argentina: evangelism in the mountain villages to the west of the agricultural lowlands. The excerpts below were selected to provide insight into the nature of Baptist evangelism and worship, with special notice paid to the changes that the new territory and peoples required. The excerpts are from the prayer letters and family correspondence written by the Gerows, sometimes in the voice of Jerry Gerow and sometimes in the voice of Janet. Although some excerpts are undated, they should be read in sequence covering the period from 1954 to 1964.

November 16, 1954—Well, we had our week of camping out at Yala! The Conference sessions took 4 days, and then some of us stayed to relax over the weekend. It was sloppy. The rainy season is upon us, but it was fun! I was elected President of the Field for 1 year, so I'll have that additional responsibility to keep me out of mischief!

Moving the work to a new people group meant having to shift the evangelistic approach.

Now, back to Pasquarello and the work. During our praying and planning together, I asked Mario Pasquarello for his counsel regarding how to begin the mountain work. He pointed out that the cultural pattern was to make contacts by "bridges." We should not begin by trying to reach the villages or to plunge in with visitation or open air work. This would be repulsive and cause violent reactions. This reminded me of the warnings we had heard from the police and officials during survey trips before furlough. They told us to stay out of the mountain villages for the people there are very suspicious of outsiders. They added that our lives would be in jeopardy. Mario suggested that he might be a bridge, since he already knew the folks up the canyon. He offered to go with me to Humahuaca and introduce me to a couple of traders (general store owners) who had bought Bibles from him. His being the "bridge" would eliminate any suspicion on their part, and then I could ask permission to sell Bibles in their stores or trading posts.

Periodically, the Indians from the mountain villages take trips down to the main canyon to deliver the skins and wool from their sheep, goats, and llamas, and trade (or swap) them for sugar, salt, rice, noodles, etc. All this is loaded on their mules, and back they go into the Andes with supplies for several more months. Since it is unwise and dangerous for us to enter their villages, we must contact them on neutral ground when they come down to where we are! Our plan includes having a stack of Bibles on the counter at the trading post, offering them for a low price to the travelers, and trusting the Lord to use His Word in their hearts and villages as they themselves take it back into the mountains.

After Juan Domingo Perón became president of Argentina (in the late 1940s), he started nationwide compulsory education. We were told it took over 2 years to send teachers, and those studying to become teachers, into every corner of the nation to register the children and warn parents of the fines for not putting their youngsters in school. So, by the time we began in the Andes there were schools in all the mountain towns. We believe the Hand of the Lord was behind this to prepare the mountain folks to read His Word! When we sold a Bible to people from way up in the hills, we knew there was someone in each home who could read!

Mario and I visited Humahuaca, the main center north of Huacalera on the old gravel Pan-American Highway. I met two store owners, Sergio Perez and Luis Rosales, both of whom had recently been led to Christ by Mario Pasquarello. Each gave us permission to sell Bibles in his store. I chose the latter because his store was larger and nearer the principal mule trails up into the mountains to the east. Luis Rosales continued to be a perfect "bridge" for our relations with the mountain folks. Miracles were beginning to happen all around us. We saw the answers to the prayers of that host of intercessors supporting us! Thank the Lord!!

Armando Morales appeared at Ontivero's store while I was selling Bibles there. He entered through the main front double door opposite where I was standing, and marched strait across the store toward me with a determined stride. I wondered what was happening; he looked so serious and huge! When he got close, I saw he had a Bible under his arm. That helped! He looked down at me and asked, "Are you the one who knows all about this Book?" My answer was, "I know something about it. Can I help you?" He replied, "I hope so. I bought this book from a little short guy (Mario Pasquarello). He said it would change my life, and it didn't work. I've come here to complain! Come on out back!" So I followed him into a huge warehouse behind the trading post. The place was piled with boxes, crates, bales of hay, and all kinds of merchandise. In one corner, there was a dusty table and a couple of chairs. "Sit down," he ordered. He pulled up the other chair and sat opposite me. He threw his Bible

The missionary appears to be misinformed, as education was already compulsory. Perón did reinforce the education law, helping to ensure more thorough nationwide access to education. Given the strong biblical approach the missionaries took to evangelism and church life, this appeared providential to them.

down on the table, raising a cloud of dust, and bellowed, "What's wrong with that Book. It didn't change my life like the guy said it would."

The Lord gave me an answer in the form of another question, "Why did your life need changing?" Then he told me of his terrible life of drunkenness, drugs, and open sin. His wife couldn't stand him any longer, and had returned to the mountain village of her youth to earn a living raising sheep. His son, who worked with him in his carpenter shop, gave up, left, and found work farther down the canyon. He began to fail his clients. He came to a place where he couldn't make 4 legs alike for a table, etc. He was a goner! When the colporteur, Pasquarello, offered him a Book that would change his life, his response was, "That is what I need!"

He explained that he had read it, but it didn't change anything. "I decided I wasn't reading it loudly enough," he said, "so I went outside the village into the desert, and screamed it, as I read, at the top of my lungs." I asked if that helped, and he sheepishly admitted that it didn't. I pointed out that how loud one reads has nothing to do with it. What was important was what it said. This Book was telling us something about Someone! I asked if he had seen the name Jesus as he read. He thought he had seen it somewhere in there. Very slowly and carefully I explained the whole gospel message to him, step by step, using his Bible, and having him read the verses. God's Spirit convicted him, and enlightened him, and led him to the place of decision. I told him Jesus was right there with us, invisibly by His Spirit, and that He had heard all our conversation. I added that Jesus Christ was clapping at the door of his heart and wanted to come in to wash away his sins and be his Savior.

He poured out his heart before the Lord, confessed his sin, and invited the Savior in. That day he was soundly converted. I was thanking God, when it dawned on me: this was our first soul in the pioneer mountain work! And less than a week from our arrival date! And we didn't have to go out looking for people. He had come to me, seeking help. Thank you, Lord! God's people were praying, and God answers prayer!! We explained to him that real change he had sought was now possible since Christ lived in him (Galatians 2:20). He readily agreed that a life with God in it should certainly be a changed life! He was satisfied and went on his way rejoicing!

Word spread rapidly that Armando had quit liquor and drugs and had opened his carpenter shop again. Unbelievable! Folks came from all over to see for themselves. When they asked what happened to him, he would give them his testimony, and then expect them to turn to the Lord immediately. If they hesitated, he would grab them by the arm and lead them a few blocks to where I was selling Bibles in the trading post and say "Here, do to him what you did to me. He needs Jesus!" Many came to the Lord through his testimony.

One day a mountaineer, traveling by mule back to Humahuaca, told Armando's wife up in the mountains about her husband's changed life. Then another, and another, brought her the story, which she found difficult to believe. She had seen him "swear off" these vices

Argentines announce their arrival at a home by clapping their hands outside the front door, not by knocking on the door or ringing a doorbell.

before and in a few days, or hours, return, like a pig to the mud! Finally curiosity got the best of her, and she traveled down to Humahuaca to see for herself. In his urging her to be saved right away, he confused her and then brought her to us as he had done to so many. We talked with her, but it was all so new and incomprehensible. At first we got nowhere.

Then, one day she showed up at our home in Huacalera. Her husband had sent her down on the morning bus, with instructions to visit us, and return north on the afternoon train. God answered prayer, opened her blinded eyes, and she came to Him in our living room. She had lunch with us, and then confessed that she could not read. She asked Janet to use the time until the train came, to teach her some verses of God's Word by heart. The picture of Janet beside her on the sofa, pouring over the Bible verses, left an indelible impression in my memory. She was bubbling over with joy when we put her on the train to return to her husband, a born again child of the same God who had transformed him!

The second profession in this pioneer work had come in the mail. A fellow picked up a tract we tossed from the car. After reading and believing it, he accepted the Lord, signed the tract, and sent it to us shortly after Armando had come to Christ! How God answered prayer!

We started regular Bible studies in that same corner of the warehouse where Armando had accepted Christ. Some of the benches used were made by him and his son in their carpenter shop. The group grew by leaps and bounds. One day a new lady entered the meeting, and all those present began to look at each other in amazement. We were puzzled until we heard that she was "one of the most devoted and faithful Roman Catholics in Humahuaca." When we asked her if she would like to decide to follow Christ, she said, "Next week." Sure enough, the following week she returned with her husband, and they both came to Christ! And this wonderful trend continues. Praise the Lord!!

The daily processions continue (since December 8 [the feast of the immaculate conception of Mary]), and pass right in front of our house. . . . They carry anywhere from one to ten images, on their shoulders, to the constant beat of drums that makes the ground tremble, and usually have a few flutes or instruments. At each street corner they release a bomb, or giant firecracker, and once in a while turn one loose right in front of our house.

The Lord continues to answer your prayers. Thursday night the RC priest's assistant (sacristan) from a mountain town northeast of Humahuaca accepted Christ in our Bible class in Humahuaca, and asked to be enrolled in the Gospel of John Correspondence Course. He, Felix Esparza, was a leader of the town and the highest authority between annual visits of the priest. He is a key person and very influential. Jerry had spoken to him at Rosales's store and tried to sell him a Bible but he refused it.

The next time the RC priest came through his town Felix asked a lot of questions and found that the priest could not give him satisfactory answers. He hurried back to Humahuaca and purchased a Bible from Rosales. He spent days comparing this Bible with his RC version. Rosales and Jerry helped him in his studies and comparisons of the versions when he came

These liturgical processions were a combination of liturgical requirement and popular religiosity. The tension and differences between the Baptists and Catholics are again obvious. Note the use of local instruments in the Catholic procession. Were Catholic practices ironically more inculturated than Baptist practices in this case?

to Humahuaca. He realized that the priest had misled him, saying the evangelical Bible was written by Martin Luther and was of the devil! In December 1955, while he was in Humahuaca purchasing supplies to take to his mountain home, Rosales persuaded him to stay for Jerry's Thursday night Bible class. That night he was saved!

His facial expression changed, and he was transformed. He asked us about leading his neighbors up in the hills to the Lord! He was thrilled to find that they could be saved by following the same steps he had just taken. From then on he never wavered. He had seen it in God's Word for himself and was completely convinced. This was the beginning of a complete spiritual revolution in that place for the Lord! Before long he had personally led two of his brothers, his father, and his best friend to the Lord. Praise Him! He was baptized in 1957 and a church was organized in his town. It gets more marvelous as time goes on. We wonder what will be next! Incidentally, on a subsequent visit of the priest he found no support or followers left there. The story he spread was that the "gospel people" [i.e., the Baptists] had ruined the place, he couldn't find a home to take him in, and he had no intentions of returning there!

The big news is our Easter Conference, the first Bible Conference ever held in this new area of CBFMS work! New believers and interested ones were invited down from the hills and surrounding towns. People came from 16 localities! The speaker was [Roque] Barroso, from Greenman's work, and hero of the film *Under the Southern Cross*. The Lord really used that dear fellow, who came to Christ in our first tent meeting in San Pedro in 1948! Hearts were melted by God's power, and 29 decisions were made of which we know. Three were by those who had already professed, but sought assurance. Some who believed were from new mountain villages, opening further doors of opportunity, and greater tasks of follow-up.

1955 And Following—Concepcion Garcia was a well-to-do mountain Indian from Santa Ana, high in the Andes between Humahuaca and Ledesma. The home-spun clothes and modest manner made one think he was living in poverty, but he wasn't. Though he had little or no cash, his real estate, cattle, sheep, mules, and horses were worth a mint of money. There were many like him in that part of the Andes. Concepcion was a deeply religious and sincere man. He had been devoted to the strange combination of decadent Roman Catholicism and raw Indian paganism, which totally surrounded him in those hills. There were spells of conviction of sin, based on his drinking, fighting, and rough life, and he was not satisfied with his total lack of assurance of ever solving the sin problem or of knowing God.

When the priest came on his annual visit to the mountains, Concepcion spoke to him about his need of assurance about his relation to God! The priest answered his question by leaving a few books for him to read. He avidly read and studied the books. One book said he should confess to the priest all that he had ever done, give account of his every step. It mentioned that he could not fool God, since He knows all about us, even the number of hairs on our head. So, sincere Concepcion began to keep a record of each step he took, moment by moment, day after day, so he could tell God about them. In no time, he lost count, and after several attempts, gave up. He even tried to count the hairs on the head of one of his sons. Before long, he abandoned that project as hopeless, and impossible. In desperation, he abandoned trying and threw himself into sin, debauchery, and even black magic.

On a trading trip to Humahuaca, a large village on the Pan American highway in the canyon, he talked with Luis Rosales, the grocer. Luis was a brand new believer. He pointed out to Concepcion that he had two problems. One was sin that was running his life because he did not know the Lord. The second problem was his saturation with Roman Catholicism. . . . Back in the hills, he pondered these things over and over. On his next trip to the canyon he tried to buy "God's Book," the Bible, without success. He found a fellow who had a New Testament and offered to pay him for it. The chap didn't want to sell it. He found the fellow had bought it in the capital city for 2 pesos. He offered him 10. The response was negative. He offered 50. Still no deal. Finally, in desperation, he offered him 500 pesos, which at that time was the price of a horse! But the fellow still would not sell it. Garcia returned to Santa Ana very sad! As time went on, his hunger for God's Book increased. In the meantime Luis had placed Bibles on his shelf in the Trading Post, and given us permission to sell Bibles in his store.

On a later trip, Concepcion Garcia bought one of those books and hurried home with his treasure to study it. And study he did, night and day! As he read "Believe on the Lord Jesus Christ, and thou shalt be saved" (Acts 16:31) and similar verses, he was deeply impressed. So he sent for his family and close relatives, told them what he had discovered in God's Book, and insisted they believe lest they go to hell! When he related all this to me, weeks later, he admitted being puzzled when pressed to explain what "believe" meant. He told them, "Well, let's just talk to God and say to Him that we believe, because He said we should believe." His family's attitude was, "Anything you say, Dad," and they all followed his suggestion.

After a while, in his total sincerity, he called them together again to consider baptism. He thought this was also important, though the details of how it should be done perplexed him. They finally agreed to all go down to the nearby mountain creek. Never having seen a baptism, and unable to find specific instructions in the part of the Bible they had read, he recalled a picture in a distant chapel of someone kneeling beside a stream. So he lined up the family on their knees beside the water, and splashed them real well. Not to be left out, he had his wife splash him also, and they returned soaked and rejoicing to the house! (Note: A few months after this, we visited their community, and saw many of them come to Christ. Later we taught them about baptism, and they were immersed! We encountered numerous cases like this, where a combination of superstition, ignorance, and a limited understanding of the Bible was combined with unbelievable desire to obey and incredible sincerity which led them to do some of the most unheard of things!)

After the episodes mentioned above, and before our first trip to Santa Ana in May, Concepcion appeared one weekend in Humahuaca with as many of his family as he could get free to accompany him. There were over a dozen of them and they had come to do whatever God wanted them to do, and do it correctly with our help! When I suggested they sit on the benches where we had our meetings, Garcia said, "No, we're going to kneel down by the benches." So they all knelt down. It took a couple of hours or more, but I did my best to be simple and stick to the Bible language and terms, letting them follow in their Bible.

I chose 5 or 6 verses from different parts of the Bible which I was in the habit of using to lead one to Christ, like "all have sinned . . . ," "wages of sin . . . ," "gift of God . . . ," etc. Would you believe it, every verse I started to quote as I went along, was finished aloud almost immediately by Concepcion! Every one! I asked him how he knew the verse and his answer consistently was, "When I read that part at home, I thought it was important, so I read it over and over until I knew it by heart!" Don't we see the finger of the Holy Spirit answering prayer, preparing hearts, teaching these hungry souls exactly the verses that would be used to lead them to the Savior! We just praised and thanked God and kept going! The whole group came to Christ that day. And the Lord put his hand on Concepcion and his son to be our guides in many of the mule trips that followed during those 9 years in the Andes. What a gem he was, a perfect companion, a very dear brother in Christ, and he became a great preacher and teacher of the Word of God.

I had exactly the same experience with Pablo Aguilar who lived many miles from Concepcion's town. He had been reading the Bible, purchased in Humahuaca where we were selling them at the Trading Post. When I led him and his wife to the Lord, Pablo quoted accurately from memory the same verses as soon as I'd mention the first couple of words. At times we felt we were "on holy ground," in the presence of the Almighty God who had prepared these hearts!

I'll never forget one of our early mule trips with Concepcion Garcia as my guide. We had trouble with the straps on the pack animals. When it first happened, we dismounted to repair one that was broken. My thought was, "I'm going to learn something. How does one fix a broken strap without a 'shop'?" Boy, did I learn something, but not about pack straps! Garcia was a new Christian, eager, sincere, and discerning. When we were about to start the job, he took off his gaucho hat, bowed his head, and muttered, "Let's commit this job to the Lord and ask him for wisdom." I thought, "What? This guy has made and fixed thousands of pack straps. What is he praying for?"

I almost slapped my own mouth to keep from saying it aloud. I confessed to God my utter lack of dependence on Him and thanked the Lord that this brother had learned well what we had taught him from God's Word. Concepcion was a perfect example of a follower of Christ who never did anything without complete dependence on his Lord. He prayed and trusted about everything, every event, every experience! I ended up asking God to make me more like Concepcion Garcia!

Through the years that followed he was used of the Lord, not only as our faithful guide for

Recurring elements of Baptist piety come together in this story: use of biblical texts in sequence to lead to a decision for Christ, a reliance upon the Scripture as the way in which salvation is revealed, and a sense that God is actively engaged in this sort of mission.

many mule trips, but as a "missionary" to reach many for Christ in the mountains. He dedicated much time to visits to isolated folk, evangelizing and teaching them, and was God's instrument in opening up the work in several localities. One time, he wrote me a letter and insisted I take a trip with him. He wanted to show me something back there in the hills. I finally consented and included this trip in my heavy schedule. It took three days to get there by mule, but we finally arrived at the area, a zone I had never visited. We were met by a group of 40 believers! Garcia had led them to Christ. They had turned from their paganism, witchcraft, and idolatry.

The story of Santa Ana is so interesting. The folks there had been reading the Bible for weeks since the first ones were brought back from their shopping trips to Humahuaca in the main canyon. The Spirit of God had begun His work in their souls. The power of God broke through during our visit, but not without our receiving a jolting cultural lesson.

We taught hymns and choruses and studies from God's Word hour after hour, from the moment we arrived, all day and late into the night each day. From the very beginning, we perceived that their hungry, prepared hearts were soaking up the truth of the gospel. We also noticed that whenever we asked for personal decisions for Christ, we drew a blank! There was no visible response. I went to my bedroll the first night perplexed and puzzled. Was there something in me that hindered God's blessing and their making decisions? I confessed, prayed, and wondered. It was the same the following day. When I asked questions, they gave the correct answers. When I asked about getting their sins forgiven, or how to get to heaven, they knew. But when I asked if they would believe and receive him as they had explained back to me, they just looked at me and at one another expressionless!

That night was rough. I poured my heart out to the Lord and pleaded for His mercy and intervention. On our third day, I realized that there were periodic "committee meetings" over in one corner of the large adobe building. There was a constant lack of formality and continuous coming and going of folks. This was normal in that mountain culture and did not detract from their attention to the studies. But these little meetings of village leaders over at the side of the room caught my attention, and made me extremely curious and apprehensive. They repeatedly looked over my way as though discussing me and what I was teaching.

I believe it was our third day there, when these leaders interrupted my teaching after one of their meetings. They marched right up to me and announced, "We have decided to follow your gospel!" My confused response was, "Who has decided?" Their answer, "Everybody!" Suddenly I realized what was happening. I had been asking them to make individual decisions, which apparently was contrary to their culture. The "committee meetings" were necessary for discussing the trends and thoughts of the people in order to arrive at a consensus that would be the group decision and to the satisfaction of all. Their returns from such get-togethers to ask further questions concerning my teaching served to clarify their thinking and facilitate sharing and finding the consensus of the group.

One can sense that even in the end the missionary still was struggling with cultural distinctions. Is it hard to imagine that, to an American sensibility, the individual decision was critical?

I asked their forgiveness for not understanding. I told them I now recognized that decisions of importance for them are made by a group, and not individually. They heaved a sigh of relief, as if to say, "The white man is catching on!" They assured me that the whole group had decided to follow Christ. Then I suggested that I would like to know that each one personally understood that he (or she) was a sinner, and that Christ died for him or her, and that each was inviting the Lord into his (or her) life. The village leader, or "chieftan," asked, "You want to talk to us one by one?" "That's right," I responded. He swung around to the entire crowd and bellowed out, "Line up!"

I'll never forget the scene that followed. I sat inside that doorway of that adobe room and looked out upon a string of Andean Indians through the patio, across the corral, and on out into the desert. It was a column of heads of families in bright colored ponchos, wives carrying babies in brilliant shawls on their backs, with young people and children tagging along. About 40 came to Christ that afternoon. Add those who had found the Savior in Humahuaca on their shopping visits, and the congregation of believers reached over 50 in Santa Ana!

The following numbered paragraphs come from a larger discussion of the characteristics of this missionary work.—Ed.

3. DON'T BELIEVE ANYTHING THE PRIEST TELLS YOU, UNLESS HE CAN SHOW YOU PROOF IN THE BIBLE! On their annual visits to the hills, the RC priests did all they could to side-track the new believers with teaching, threats, enticements, and any means they could employ. We taught our folks to use the Bible with them, which proved to be very effective. We heard some of the complaints of the priests (second hand) when they returned to the cities after visiting the mountains. One remark had to do with starting to teach the R[oman] Catholics their Bible so they could stand effectively against the Evangelical believers. One mentioned that the "gospel people" [i.e., the Baptists] had ruined a certain town. No one there welcomed the priest anymore! That town was entirely committed to God's message and Word! Whenever I taught the village believers the capitalized words with which we begin section 3, I always added, "And don't you believe anything I tell you, unless I can show you the truth in the Bible!" What excitement, when they would hold me to that, or challenge me with those words. We loved it! They were learning the basics!

4. WHAT ABOUT SUNDAY SCHOOLS IN THE MOUNTAIN CHURCHES? Well, we had an interesting cultural pattern in the Andes. Those folks do everything as family or clan units. That's the way they run their farms and lives, make decisions, go to church, and do everything: side by side as an entire family. It is most wholesome and necessary to them! This, incidentally, is more like the culture we see in Bible times in this respect, than the U.S.A. culture today. That is one reason we did not departmentalize the work at the beginning. A second reason is we

were determined in the pioneer phase of the work to stick to the Word of God in every detail on which the Bible spoke. Missions are God's work, not man's. World evangelization is God's project, not ours. Therefore, when His Word indicates how to reach the world and do mission work, that has priority. At the same time, when He explicitly tells us what to do, or not do, we must be attentive and obedient.

Let's put it this way: whatever is biblical, we must obey without argument or compromise. Whatever is anti-biblical, we must refuse and reject always. Whatever is extra-biblical must be considered by its merits in each case. Sunday School is extra-biblical, as is youth work and women's meetings. They are neither right nor wrong by biblical standards. At a committee meeting in one of the provincial capitals, I was sharing God's blessing in the new pioneer work in the mountains, and my colleagues could hardly believe what was happening up there. They commented that they would like to see it with their own eyes. I invited them to go on a mountain trip with me. Walter Hoops later took me up on the offer and accompanied me to Santa Ana. When he saw people gathering, and all the children coming with them, he said (always in Spanish in front of the nationals!), "You must have a great Sunday School here!" One of the new believers asked him to repeat that. After hearing the remark a second time, the new believer pushed his Bible toward Walt, and asked, "Show me what chapter that is in!"

I was delighted. This chap had caught on! Everything must be checked by the Book! That is basic! However, as time passed, and contacts were made with city churches in regional conferences and associations, the moment arrived when they began to employ some of the extra-biblical ideas that have been used and blessed of the Lord. At the beginning of the work in the mountains (in a culture where they do everything as a family unit), it would have been disastrous to break up the household. Now they have slowly become a part of a larger evangelical culture, and most of the mountain churches, if not all, have S[unday] S[chool], women's groups, youth work, and so on.

In the name of Christianity, the Romanists have constantly opposed the simple message of God's Word here in the Humahuaca canyon. In one case, half-wild dogs were ordered to attack Jerry for offering a tract! Others threatened to club him, if he tried to visit them again! One family planned to throw kerosene on him and ignite it! One of our new believers was attacked by several men with knives who, in the name of Rome, were determined to do away with this hated Evangelical. God miraculously delivered him from a terrible death! Another new follower of Christ had his throat laid open with a straight razor by a drunken barber, eager to put an end to the "new religion" that had entered the area! The wounded one was rescued by old drinking buddies, who also gave their own blood as transfusions to keep him alive. One dear orphan girl, who worked for a druggist, asked for time off to attend our Sunday meeting and was immediately fired.

A year ago there were no Evangelicals in Santa Ana and no Bibles. We have visited them only on one occasion. These dear folks have no gospel background; they are babes in Christ. It is a miracle that any of them follow on in the face of the enemy's aggression! Yes, it is the miracle power of the precious Holy Spirit, sealing and caring for His own. Many, many of them are standing tall and true, thank the Lord! In fact, they are made much stronger in the Lord by these senseless attacks. Please join us in bearing them up in intercessory prayer.

Our week in Santa Ana was most impressive. Months ago when we taught them of the scriptural meaning and practice of baptism by immersion, the new believers immediately began to plan for such a service in their town. The problem in Santa Ana is water! In that high mountain desert, the whole town lives from two trickling springs! Some families have to carry water great distances from one of those small sources to their homes. One of these tiny streams, about 8 inches wide and less than four inches deep, passes near the home of Concepcion Garcia. He obtained permission to draw water from that trickling stream for certain limited times. The new Christians hauled bags of cement on pack animals from Humahuaca (two days), dug a tremendous baptistery in Concepcion's yard, lined it with stones and cement, and began filling it, weeks before our November visit.

> Because of the lack of water, the commitment to immersion baptism as the biblical way of baptizing required some creative improvising.

The baptismal service was extremely impressive and precious. 9 candidates gave beautiful testimonies of their finding and trusting Christ and confirmed their faith with this lovely step of obedience to Him. I was deeply affected when I learned that this was the first time some of them had ever been submerged in water, and the women, especially, were terrified at the thought. But they bravely did it for Jesus! Partial sponge baths is all they know in that cold, dry climate. Being bodily in water would be related to getting caught in a flash flood or some such disaster. Their remarkable response to God's Word, in obedience and trust, was a real lesson to us! We also studied the Word with them concerning the broken bread and the cup and together celebrated their first Lord's Supper. What a sacred experience that was! Then there were times of special prayer, seeking God's will and plan, and discovering His choices for the leadership of the new church. It was some week!

The work in Santa Ana is going real well. During the two days there, 13 more were baptized, bringing the total of full members to 22. Four more came to the Lord also. The numbers in the meetings packed the spacious room we used. They are on the verge of building a "temple" there. The foundation is already prepared. It will be much larger than their present meeting place, and off by itself in a neutral area, away from the stigma of being part of a private home. Those dear mountain people are so sincere and trusting. It was a great privilege to be present with them around the Lord's table. Can you imagine 20 taking part and many others silently watching, while we remembered the sacrifice of the Savior for us, in a place where there was not one believer a year ago! We certainly have much for which to praise the Lord!!

April 5, 1956—The Easter Conference was wonderful! We could write a book about it! We began Thursday, and none of the speakers arrived until Friday afternoon! So Gerow had to carry on alone, trusting that relief would come. Cortez never did get there. Word came Thursday night that [Roque] Barroso had arrived in Jujuy, couldn't get tickets for Humahuaca (sold out!), and had returned to San Pedro! Bob Hall, bless his heart, offered to drive to S.P. He left 4:30 a.m. on Friday to get Barroso. Maldonado finally arrived by car about 3 p.m. Friday. All through the days of conference, Janet worked like a slave with the church women, cooking over an open fire in the patio of the Gospel Hall. They fed some 175 or more who attended. We calculate that well over 200 took advantage of the meetings, though all did not eat there. It was a three-ring circus, believe me! We had many sleeping in the auditorium, and all over the place. We spent the first night there ourselves, but afterwards commuted, since Greenman arrived, and offered to keep an eye on things at night. Our nights were short at home, and wore the kiddies down, but they were so good through it all. The blessings way outweighed the difficulties and inconveniences.

There were 29 localities represented (16 last year). Folks came from San Pedro, Pichanal, Calilegua, La Esperanza, even Salta, and many of the mountain towns. Tears of joy flowed as we delivered them from the slavery of sin. 11 were baptized from the Humahuaca work, and we had our first Lord's Supper there. What a precious service that was, hardly a dry eye. The Lord's presence and power was so apparent during those days; real revival seemed to begin in our hearts, and has continued. Praise His Name! There were also 12 clear cut decisions for Christ.

As told in the prayer letter, written this a.m., I went to Humahuaca Monday morning to help clean up. I found about 30 gathered, singing, worshipping, and praising the Lord for the blessings of His presence. They just couldn't face the fact that it was over, and [they] would not quit. We continued our praise service until well after the noon hour. When we finally broke up, they said it was too long until our regular Thursday Bible study and prayer meeting, so planned one for Tuesday evening. This became a weekly service! We thank God for what He is doing in Humahuaca, and in our hearts! We could go on for pages, but paper and time are running out!! So much for now. The family join me in sending our love. D. [Jerry Gerow].

First Week in May, 1957—The Easter Conference was wonderful! 31 localities represented; 31 baptisms; 16 professions of faith, etc.! Samuel Lopez came to Christ on our first visit to Caspalá, at the end of 1954. Several months later, his wife was baptized, but at that time he was still a slave to the drug, cocaine, in the coca leaves. He appeared at this conference, 82 years old, after traveling a day and a half from home. Some of the trip was on a mule but much of it by foot. He gave a glowing testimony of Christ's victory over coca in his life, and was one of those baptized! The evangelistic team from B[uenos] A[ires] was just great with all their wonderful music, painting, and powerful preaching.

The conference caused quite a stir in quiet Humahuaca! We obtained permission and put up powerful loudspeakers. The whole town had to hear it, even with their doors shut. The rig rocked the town with its power! After the first "broadcast," the priest sent a hot letter to the mayor, demanding that he rescind the permission, or face a public demonstration against him in the plaza. The mayor came to us and pleaded with us to be nice and quiet. We told him to show some backbone and stand for the rights the law provides: liberty for all, etc.

December 1957—One of our deaconesses from Humahuaca went to Jujuy to work, and 2 months later returned a "wild Pentecostal"! Another of "them" came back with her and they caused an awful fuss among the believers. They visited them all, telling them they were lost after all. . . .

The feast of Epiphany, January 6, has traditionally commemorated the coming of the Magi since the last patristic period in Western churches.

November 1959 [**This entry was made when the Gerows were in the US.**]—Our memories go back to the Christmas season in Argentina. The Argentines, when they were not affected by foreign influences of movies, TV, videos, and books, gave their gifts on January 6 instead of December 25. To us this is very significant in light of Latin American history and culture. That date is the Day of the Magi, the Kings, or the Wise Men [i.e., the feast of Epiphany]. That is the moment when men gave gifts to Jesus, typical R[oman] Catholic slant of human works for God! Christmas is our day of gifts because on that date God gave His Son for our salvation, the perfect picture of grace, in contrast to works. So the gift of His Son, and the gift of salvation, is the basis of our giving at that season. The basis for the Latin American's giving was the visit of the Magi with gifts of gold, incense, and myrrh for God in the manger!

January 6 would be a good day to pray in a special way for Latin America, asking God to open their blind eyes to see His grace and accept His gift of salvation in Christ! Jerry, for the Gerows.

Notes on Church Buildings (written for CBFMS Field Conference [1962])—On this subject, the best illustrative material we can offer is from our work in the Andes mountains. We saw that work start from scratch and are familiar with all the steps. In all seven of our organized churches, the work was begun in private homes, "the church in thy house" sort of situation. Even in Huacalera/San José area where we live, the work began in a national's home, not in the home of a foreign missionary!

Humahuaca is the largest town on the Pan American Highway (gravel) between the provincial capital and the Bolivian border. We began meetings there in the warehouse of a general store or "trading post." As the Christian store owner became more assertive as "owner" of the work (since we met under his roof), we challenged the group with the idea of a neutral meeting place. They immediately acted favorably. Based on our teaching from day one, they never expected the mission or missionary to provide or pay for a place for them. They moved from the warehouse and rented a large building. From the first month they paid all the rent, which would be comparable to any business building rental in town.

During our furlough they moved to a more expensive rental building nearer the center of town without missionary suggestion or help! Today they are about to purchase their own property and adapt the building on it for a church and educational plant. They do not expect missionary help financially. They rejoice in this way of proving their love for the Lord (2 Corinthians 9), and they are giving their life (represented by their earnings) while the missionary gives his life for the Lord in other ways. They have shown real maturity in the discernment and understanding of these matters.

In two villages the believers outgrew the homes in which they met and, without even advising the missionary, built a large neutral meeting place where they gather at present. Other groups either have built or are building now. Many believe a neutral site is preferable to a private home and that invited friends are more likely to attend there. In every case, the initiative and footing of all the bills have come from the national believers. In most cases the building has been expensive in comparison to the economic level of the church people. They always wish to give the Lord the best! In some cases building involved hiring trucks to haul supplies and materials. In others it was done by train along the Pan-American highway, or by lengthy and numerous mule trips in the hills. But never have they even hinted that the missionary should pay, or provide his vehicle. (In some cases we have offered help in a normal and brotherly fashion, and had it accepted. In others we have worked side by side with them. But they never expected nor demanded more and more.) I think this is a reflection of the teaching from the first day the gospel entered the mountain field.

The believers were taught full responsibility, financial and otherwise, and complete control and accountability under God from the very beginning. As new believers learned to carry the full burden of accountability to God in every area of their lives, the missionaries guided them through teaching and close supervision. As they learned to lean more on the Lord and the Word for themselves in all decision making in the work, the missionaries' active part in leading and teaching decreased. The national believers knew that they were completely responsible before God from the very beginning.

As other groups become organized churches, we don't anticipate any problems concerning church buildings. They already know that such details are to be solved by them in unity before the Lord and His Word. Also these groups have the splendid example of the other churches of the area which have dealt with these matters successfully and efficiently without financial help from missionaries or the Mission Society. C. D. Gerow, Dec. 17, 1962.

Perhaps the right behavior comes from the missionaries' teaching, but it might come from intrinsic cultural values within the converts. In what ways might the sending missionary agency's policy document create a presumption in its missionaries that their new converts would be demanding?

The same day that Ferguson and I left for Santa Ana, Janet and Hazel were faced with a traumatic experience. They received a telegram at Huacalera that Nemesio Cruz had died, and they should go immediately to Humahuaca. So off they went (Janet had been up since

4:30 a.m. to see me off) and, upon arrival, heard that Nemesio died way up in the mountains where he had gone to teach school. They had to get a truck to fetch his body, and most of the key men were in the hills with us on our trips. Salas and Rosales finally went. Janet and Hazel kept the believers calm as they showed up as the news spread.

At last, the body arrived. They worked all night in preparations for the service and burial. They tried to bed Jimmy and Sandy down somewhere to get some sleep. Janet and Hazel and the two kiddies went to Huacalera for a bit of sleep after daylight and returned to Humahuaca for the burial later in the day. At the cemetery Nemesio's wife asked for a chance to pray and led in a strong clear voice a victorious prayer of praise for the Lord and His perfect will. All said it was a most triumphant testimony. Nemesio was one of the four elders of the Humahuaca church and a terrific witness.

In Salta there was a church split! Praise the Lord!

It was planned this way! A new church was planted in a distant corner of the city by dividing the present congregation according to the geographical distribution of the members' homes. The result is a solid testimony in a new area of Salta!

This was *not* the normal procedure followed in the planting of over 30 churches in north Argentina by CBFMS! Usually, in new areas the work began with evangelism by visitation, tract distribution, Bible sales, personal work, radio, open air meetings, or preaching in a tent, rented hall, or a home. Then came the task of follow-up of converts and bringing them together in a group. Our aim was to obey Christ's commission, "teaching them to observe all things whatsoever I have commanded you" (Matthew 28:20), which includes the formation of a local church. Candidates were trained and baptized. The new group was stabilized through teaching. Lay officers were elected and baptisms were followed by the Lord's Supper. The missionary training and supervision continued while the group learned to be Christ-centered, self-governing, self-supporting, self-propagating, and competent to teach one another (Rom. 15:14 and Ephesians 3 and 4). Fellowship with other churches of like doctrine and practice was recommended. Then the missionary gradually withdrew his active part and supervision of the congregation. Withdrawal completed, the foreign missionary would be available for counsel and help for limited periods of time at the invitation of the new church, which was now on its own under God.

It sounds easy, and looks smooth on paper! But there are at least [two] major problems to face in this process:

1. MEETING PLACE—In the city of Tucumán, at the south end of the CBFMS field, property prices have skyrocketed. The church is small. An upper class well-to-do believer has invited the church to meet in her home—a second floor apartment. Such arrangements nearly always impair growth and blessings, either because the host feels an unwholesome ownership of the work, or because some hesitate to go into "so-and-so's home." A neutral

meeting place, if available and affordable, eliminates many hindering prejudices and contributes to the normal growth of the church.

2. CULTURAL AND CLASS PATTERNS—The Jujuy work, like other city efforts, suffers from trying to unite people from widely varied classes and castes into one congregation. The missionary deals with each as an equal, from a high society woman to a mason's helper. But the uncomfortable feeling in each other's presence is shared by all in the meeting. The sculptor from the School of Fine Arts in Barcelona, an ex-diplomat from Bolivia, a public accountant, store owners, clerks, and peons (low-class day-laborers) are all thrown together in church. Socially, in everyday life, they are separated into caste-like groups, divisions strictly adhered to! This problem must be addressed and a solution found. In one city this is cared for by having more than one congregation, and all of them united at the Association of Churches level.

Another phase of the problem is the fact that the idea of "fellowship" was completely foreign to the people of north Argentina, especially in the Andes. In their culture there was no such thing as a gathering to enjoy friendship. All social get-togethers are to escape reality and indulge in personal enjoyment for selfish benefits, using drinks, promiscuity, and drugs together. At the beginning, the believers could not understand any need for continued meetings or the permanent establishing of a congregation.

Given the stridency and broad generalization of the missionary's comment, is it fair to wonder about its accuracy?

Stories from Tent Meetings in Cerrillos, Salta, April 1964—The visiting Pocket Testament League (PTL) Team gave our meetings a perfect "kick-off"! With their sound truck they announced the meeting all over town, offering free movies. In spite of the rain, a great crowd gathered, and no one was disappointed. The program was wonderful, and all enjoyed it. We followed, after they left for San Pedro, with our slides and chalk talks each night and had a good turnout. About the 4th night, the local priest had about all he could take. He had a sound truck out to announce his movie, *The Lost World*. We wondered what would happen. A good group showed up at the tent, and all seemed normal until someone said aloud, "Let's hurry up now because we want to see the priest's film afterward!" All went well. The following night we had a fine crowd. We asked some of the children about the priest's movie, and they just grunted and mumbled, "We couldn't get in. He charged admission!"

Teresita—She was a University student. Her mother found the Savior in the tent and then her [brother] also. They invited Teresita to attend. She finally did, arriving late and arguing vehemently afterward in favor of her religion.

The last night of the tent campaign arrived. Her mother and brother were there as usual, but not Teresita. There was a fiesta and procession of the Roman Catholics that evening, and she couldn't miss that! The pounding of hundreds of feet was heard as they passed the tent only minutes before we went to start our last meeting. Two of those feet were Teresita's!

Then something happened! As though moved by some unseen power, Teresita decided to leave the procession and enter the tent, inviting several of her friends to accompany her. They marched in and filled about a bench and a half toward the back of the tent. They sang from the chorus sheets and paid attention to the slides and message until something else unusual happened. In marched a woman in the middle of the message looking for her daughter. Unceremoniously, she succeeded in hauling some of the girls out. Several more followed, and then there sat Teresita all alone on the end of a bench. She listened attentively to the preaching but made no decision when others accepted Christ. Later that night she returned to the tent in the pouring rain crying her eyes out. She had run from her home with no umbrella nor coat. She admitted being under crushing conviction of sin and anxious to know her sins were forgiven. She just had to settle it, but "Is it necessary that I change my religion? I'm Roman Catholic. I love my religion. I have to receive Christ, but I want to know if that involves a change of religion."

I explained that it is not a matter of changing religion; no religion saves. It is a matter of receiving Christ personally and establishing a relationship with Him through faith. Then I added, "Once you really know Christ personally as your Savior, the things that have meant so much to you will probably fade and disappear as unnecessary. He will mean everything and supply everything. Christ will be all you need! You will be satisfied with Him and will be content to see other former beliefs drop off. It will be okay with you that some things disappear!" Her puzzled expression was replaced with a peaceful smile, and she opened her heart to Christ and found salvation and joy in Him.

One night a fellow came forward with others at the invitation but later confessed that he had not prayed to receive Christ with the group. He admitted he was moved by the message, then rather hurriedly said "Adios" [goodbye], and added, "I'll be back."

A few nights later, he showed up with his wife. At the close, I talked with him in the aisle and asked if he had made a decision. His answer was, "Not yet, but I am ready now. I brought my wife to do it with me. We are both ready!" The Spirit of God had prepared them; they confessed their sin and received the Lord. As we said "Adios" that night, he remarked, "Now our home life should be different. We had our problems, but expect Jesus to change our home now." All reports indicated that Christ made a real difference in that home because both lives were now His!

A poorly dressed chap stood in the back of the tent one night. During our "chalk talk" (presenting the gospel), he inched forward and finally sat down on the end of a bench. At the close, he came to the front and asked if he could buy a Bible which had been offered during the meeting. When asked why he wanted a Bible, he explained that two Bolivian laborers, who work on the same ranch with him, had given him a Gospel of John that they obtained at the tent meetings. He said he had read it through. He had asked his friends where he could find out more about Jesus and salvation, and they suggested the tent meetings.

"I have not been able to get to the meetings until tonight. I am deeply impressed by the contents of that Book of John!" The church elder, José Copa, in charge of Bible sales, brought him one and told him it would be 80 pesos. Crestfallen, he admitted he only had 50. Copa asked, "You have read John?" "Yes," he said. "All of it!" "Did you enjoy it?" "Yes." "Did you understand it?" "Yes, it was wonderful. It tells of Jesus and His power and His message!"

Copa continued, "Would you like to know that Jesus Christ personally, the one who walked among men, and went to the cross, for your salvation?" His affirmative answer led to a conversation which ended in his finding the Savior! Copa sold him the Bible for 50 pesos. He left the tent rejoicing and standing tall with the Book tucked under his arm!

The whole town knew how many hundreds had taken the Gospel of John the night the PTL truck had announced and distributed them.

The PTL meeting in the Jujuy suburb, Ciudad de Nieva, had a visit from the RC priest. He came during the film and complained because the sound truck announcement before the meeting had interfered with his chapel service. He admitted there were only 5 or 6 in the chapel, but they heard of the free movies from the circulating truck, and left to see what was going on. He said PTL had no right to woo his faithful ones away. Moises explained it was just an invitation, that they had come voluntarily just as the priest himself had, and any could leave at any time, etc.

It was a great meeting with almost 600 present, including the priest! Many signed up to follow Christ and to do the Correspondence Course. Some even showed up at a local believer's home on occasion to ask for help in the Bible Course. The priest took the Gospel of John and apparently read it, for later he gave permission to his flock to read it! When the PTL Team had a meeting in the Normal School (a branch of one of the Argentine Universities), that priest was there through the whole meeting, and was very friendly afterwards, though not about to be converted, I guess!

WORSHIP TEXTS

Texts of Some of the Most-Loved Hymns Used by Baptists in Northwest Argentina

The following five hymns were some of the favorites of the Ledesma Baptists. They would have been well known among North American evangelicals, too. Note the strong emphasis upon Jesus Christ in the hymns, especially his saving invitation and mission. All five are known as "gospel songs" and were written by American or British Christians in the late nineteenth or early twentieth centuries.

Jesus Is Tenderly Calling Thee Home
By Fanny Crosby

This song was popular in the United States at the time. It exemplifies how strongly the worship piety is attached to the person of Jesus Christ. When sung as a concluding song in a service, it could set the feeling that the sinner was being directly addressed by Jesus.

Verse 1   Jesus is tenderly calling thee home—calling today, calling today;
Why from the sunshine of love wilt thou roam, farther and farther away?

Refrain:

Calling today, calling today; Jesus is calling, is tenderly calling today.

Verse 2   Jesus is calling the weary to rest—calling today, calling today;
Bring him thy burden and thou shalt be blest; he will not turn thee away.

Refrain

Verse 3   Jesus is waiting, O come to him now—waiting today, waiting today;
         Come with thy sins, at his feet lowly bow; come, and no longer delay.

Refrain

Verse 4   Jesus is pleading, O list to his voice—hear him today, hear him today;
         They who believe on his name shall rejoice; quickly arise and obey.

Refrain

Thou Didst Leave Thy Throne

By Emily E. S. Elliott

Verse 1   Thou didst leave Thy throne and Thy kingly crown,
         When Thou camest to earth for me;
         But in Bethlehem's home was there found no room
         For Thy holy nativity.

Refrain:

         O come to my heart, Lord Jesus,
         There is room in my heart for Thee.

Verse 2   Heaven's arches rang when the angels sang,
         Proclaiming Thy royal degree;
         But of lowly birth didst Thou come to earth,
         And in great humility.

Refrain

Verse 3   The foxes found rest, and the birds their nest
         In the shade of the forest tree;
         But Thy couch was the sod, O Thou Son of God,
         In the deserts of Galilee.

Refrain

Verse 4   Thou camest, O Lord, with the living Word,

That should set Thy people free;

But with mocking scorn and with crown of thorn,

They bore Thee to Calvary.

Refrain

Verse 5   When the heav'ns shall ring, and her choirs shall sing,

At Thy coming to victory,

Let Thy voice call me home, saying "Yet there is room,

There is room at My side for thee."

My heart shall rejoice, Lord Jesus,

When Thou comest and callest for me.

The Ninety and Nine

By Elizabeth C. Clephane

This hymn, based on the parable in Luke 15:4–7, reflects the deep commitment to personal evangelization that the Baptists saw in Christ and wished to imitate. To seek and save the lost both comforted and challenged them.

Verse 1   There were ninety and nine that safely lay

In the shelter of the fold.

But one was out on the hills away,

Far off from the gates of gold.

Away on the mountains wild and bare.

Away from the tender Shepherd's care.

Away from the tender Shepherd's care.

Verse 2   "Lord, Thou hast here Thy ninety and nine;

Are they not enough for Thee?"

But the Shepherd made answer: "This of Mine

Has wandered away from Me;

And although the road be rough and steep,

I go to the desert to find My sheep,

I go to the desert to find My sheep."

Verse 3 But none of the ransomed ever knew

How deep were the waters crossed;

Nor how dark was the night the Lord passed through

Ere He found His sheep that was lost.

Out in the desert He heard its cry,

Sick and helpless and ready to die;

Sick and helpless and ready to die.

Verse 4 "Lord, whence are those blood drops all the way

That mark out the mountain's track?"

"They were shed for one who had gone astray

Ere the Shepherd could bring him back."

"Lord, whence are Thy hands so rent and torn?"

"They are pierced tonight by many a thorn;

They are pierced tonight by many a thorn."

Verse 5 And all through the mountains, thunder riven

And up from the rocky steep,

There arose a glad cry to the gate of Heaven,

"Rejoice! I have found My sheep!"

And the angels echoed around the throne,

"Rejoice, for the Lord brings back His own!

Rejoice, for the Lord brings back His own!"

Only Believe (Fear Not, Little Flock)

By Paul Rader

Verse 1 Fear not, little flock, from the cross to the throne,

From death into life He went for His own;

All power in earth, all power above,

Is given to Him for the flock of His love.

Refrain:

> Only believe, only believe;
> All things are possible, only believe,
> Only believe, only believe;
> All things are possible, only believe.

Verse 2   Fear not, little flock, He goeth ahead,
             Your Shepherd selecteth the path you must tread;
             The waters of Marah He'll sweeten for thee,
             He drank all the bitter in Gethsemane.

Refrain

Verse 3   Fear not, little flock, whatever your lot,
             He enters all rooms, "the doors being shut";
             He never forsakes, He never is gone,
             So count on His presence in darkness and dawn.

Refrain

Take My Life and Let It Be
By Frances Havergal

Verse 1   Take my life, and let it be
             Consecrated, Lord, to Thee;
             Take my moments and my days,
             Let them flow in ceaseless praise.
             Let them flow in ceaseless praise.

Verse 2   Take my hands, and let them move
             At the impulse of Thy love;
             Take my feet, and let them be
             Swift and beautiful for Thee.
             Swift and beautiful for Thee.

Verse 3 Take my voice, and let me sing

Always, only, for my King;

Take my lips, and let them be

Filled with messages from Thee.

Filled with messages from Thee.

Verse 4 Take my silver and my gold:

Not a mite would I withhold;

Take my intellect, and use

Ev'ry pow'r as Thou shalt choose.

Ev'ry pow'r as Thou shalt choose.

Verse 5 Take my will, and make it Thine,

It shall be no longer mine;

Take my heart, it is Thine own,

It shall be Thy royal throne.

It shall be Thy royal throne.

Verse 6 Take my love, my Lord, I pour

At Thy feet its treasure store;

Take myself, and I will be,

Ever, only, all for Thee.

Ever, only, all for Thee.

Source: All these hymns are in the public domain.

Examples of Worship Choruses Written by Argentine Baptists

The following songs were composed by Argentine Baptists in the twentieth century. They were included in a songbook compiled by Ronald Olson for use in his church. Like the hymns above, they show a worship devotion that focuses on Jesus Christ. The benefits and hopes of knowing him are a common theme. Choruses like these would have been combined with English-written choruses translated into Spanish as well as hymns translated into Spanish to form the basic song repertoire for Argentine Baptist congregations.

You're Walking through the World

By Roque Barroso

This song by one of the Argentine preachers asked the fundamental question that drove the Baptists' sense of mission. This was the question they asked in one-on-one evangelism, in preaching, in Bible studies, and in song texts.

You're walking through the world

Without seeing where you're going.

Why don't you receive Christ

And so become happy?

With Christ guiding your life

Your being will be transformed

Because he will give you eternal life

And an inexpressible joy in your soul

That will last forever and ever.

Christian Youth Are Marching

By Carim Morcos (elder and lay pastor in Tucumán)

Verse 1   Christian youth are marching, marching;

Christian youth are marching to the heavenly kingdom.

Whoever wants to join in

Let him/her believe, believe;

Whoever wants to join in

Let him believe in the Lord Jesus.

Chorus:

Faith that conquers the world,

His word says it clearly.

Faith that conquers the world,

Jesus, Son of God.

Verse 2   If you follow the way, never, never;

If you follow the way, you'll never be lost.

Whoever receives Jesus,

Always, always;

Whoever receives Jesus,

Will always pour out love.

Chorus

Verse 3 If you have a doubt, come to Christ;

If you have a doubt, come to Christ and doubt no more.

If you lack conviction

Come, serve Christ.

If you lack conviction,

Serve Christ and you'll have it.

Chorus

Love

By *los jóvenes de Tucumán* (the youth group of Tucumán)

Love, love, love, love,

Brother, rejoice, love your neighbor

As a brother. God is love.

Love, love, love!

(repeat)

Note the simplicity of structure and message in this song. Can you think of an old praise chorus in English with the same dual simplicities?

When I Cross the River

By *los jóvenes de Tucumán* (the youth group of Tucumán)

When I cross the river, (repeat)

I will not fear. (repeat)

Jesus guides my boat and I will not fear. (repeat)

He guides my boat and I will not fear. (repeat)

When I arrive at the shore, (repeat)

God will be waiting. (repeat)

And he will sustain me in his strong arms. (repeat)

He will sustain me forever. (repeat)

The Day Will Arrive

By *los jóvenes de Tucumán* (the youth group of Tucumán)

In contrast to some of the songs in this collection, which are named aptly "choruses," because that is the only part of the song there is, this song has a more traditional form of a hymn with multiple verses.

Verse 1   The day will arrive in which I will see
          Jesus my Savior,
          And I will be really close to him
          To worship him with all my being.

Verse 2   The day will arrive, we will rejoice
          Up there in heaven, and we will sing
          New songs to God the Father.
          All glory be to him.

Verse 3   Yes, it will arrive, I'm sure.
          How will it be to be there:
          To feel only love and peace,
          And a joy that fills my soul.

Verse 4   I'm here, just waiting
          For you, Lord, to decide to come,
          To be able to say this:
          I'm ready to depart.

A Heart That Praises

By *los jóvenes de Tucumán* (the youth group of Tucumán)

A heart that praises God
Cannot be sad. (repeat)
That's why I sing and worship my Christ.
A heart that praises God
Cannot be sad.

Peace, What a Peace!

By *los jóvenes de Tucumán* (the youth group of Tucumán)

Chorus:

Peace, what a peace! that Jesus gave me,

When he saved me, and came into my heart.

Verse 1 People negotiate in order

To purchase peace,

But they always fail.

They will never find it.

Verse 2 When people finally reach

Peace in their hearts,

They will give the world

The peace that they yearn for today.

Testimonial songs like these, describing the experience of accepting Christ, have been a common element in evangelical worship.

Source: Ronald Olson, compiler, *Cantemos* (Salta, Argentina, n.d.). The choruses are #166 (p. 53), #200 (pp. 69–70), #222 (p. 82), #236 (p. 88), #255 (pp. 95–96), #262 (p. 98), #266 (p. 99) in this collection, respectively.

Sermons

The distinctive quality of a Baptist perspective can be heard in the following three sermon out-lines used by Ronald Olson in his Argentine work. Note the close attention paid to biblical texts to weave them together to form a coherent message. The same focus on Christ seen in the musical texts (pp. 94, 100) continues in these sermons. The messages reflect Olson's vocation to teach the new believers in his church.

Outline of Ronald Olson's Sermon on the Lord's Supper

The sermon on the Lord's Supper initially reflects Olson's desire to distinguish his Baptist perspective on the communion element from any carryover Catholic piety that his parishioners might have had about the bread literally becoming the body of Christ. After that beginning of negation, however, he is eager to outline the dynamic symbolic qualities of the bread as it points to the nature of the church as Christ's body and then to the wonder of the incarnation.

THIS IS MY BODY

1 Corinthians 11:24

Introduction: The Son of God, Jesus Christ, had a physical, human body. John 1:1–14.
1 Timothy 3:16. God was manifest in the flesh.
Galatians 4:4. God sent his Son, born of a woman.
1 Timothy 2:5. [There is] only one Mediator between God and man, Jesus Christ the man.

There are three ways in which we can marvel at the words of Christ: "This is my body."

I. "THIS IS MY BODY" in the Lord's Supper. 1 Corinthians 11:24

    1. This is not his actual body, literally, but it is a symbol of his body.

        I am the Door.

        I am the Way.

        I am the Vine.

        I am the Living Water.

        I am the Bread of Life, etc.

We have pictures of our five children on the wall. When our friends visit us and see the pictures, we say: "These are my children." [Editor's note: Olson uses this example to show that the language of "the body of Christ" isn't literal, just as the pictures of his children aren't literally them, even though he refers to them that way.]

    2. What is the message of this symbol for us believers?

        a. It symbolizes the past: it is a memorial of his death (vs. 24).

        b. It symbolizes the present: Christ is with us right now (vs. 26).

        c. It symbolizes the future: "until I come" (vs. 26).

II. "THIS IS MY BODY": the Church of Jesus Christ

    1. One body. Ephesians 1:22–23 and 5:30.

    2. Each one of us is an individual member. 1 Corinthians 12:27.

    What are the results of understanding and expressing this?

        a. Love. Ephesians 5:29a–30.

        b. Sympathy. 1 Corinthians 12:26–27.

        c. Respect. 1 Corinthians 12:21–22; Hebrews 13:7, 17.

        d. Submission. Submit to one another.

III. "THIS IS MY BODY": the body of each believer. 1Corinthians 6:20

    1. The miracle of the incarnation of Christ. Galatians 4:4; Isaiah 9:6.

    2. [Is there] an even greater miracle? Galatians 4:6 and 4:19: "the pain of childbirth, until the nature of Christ is formed in you." Galatians 2:20; 1:16.

    3. We in Christ: 2 Corinthians 5:17. Christ in us: 2 Corinthians 13:5. It is Paul's prayer for the believers in Ephesians 3:17–19.

    4. The glorious hope: Colossians 1:27; John 14:23; Isaiah 57:15.

Distinguishing between literal and symbolic was important for weaning the Argentine Baptists from Catholic roots. Popular Catholic religiosity would have emphasized a more literalistic approach to the sacrament.

———————

Source: Used and replicated by permission of Ronald Olson.

Outline of Ronald Olson's Sermon on Baptism

While the outline of this baptism sermon prevents us from knowing exactly what Olson said, we can see key touchstones for his theology of baptism. Olson's points seem to be reflective of Baptist history and thought, which conservative Baptists like Olson would likely have traced to Anabaptist principles and practices.

Like their Anabaptist forebears, the earliest Baptists were a diverse body of dissenters from England who were willing to separate from any establishment that threatened religious freedom or interfered with biblical principles: this was presumably the Catholic Church for the Argentine natives to whom Olson preached. Anabaptists would also have held tightly to the voluntary nature of baptism. For Anabaptists, baptism was like religion. Religion had to be voluntary to be valid, and the same was true of baptism. The voluntary nature of baptism was closely connected to early Baptists' desires to have a church of "true Christians," individuals baptized only after they had become believers—not a moment before.

Readers may notice that Olson's sermon outline is alliterated. Alliteration is a common preaching technique among conservative Baptist preachers. This literary technique has been, and continues to be, a way for unscripted (or extempore) preachers to remember their sermon points. It also serves as a helpful tool for unbelievers to remember sermons they hear, which are presumably their gateway to salvation.

Readers may also notice that Olson's sermon outline uses only texts from the New Testament. Most Baptists believe baptism originated in and was solely a New Testament practice. Furthermore, the Scripture passages Olson uses emphasize the example or words of Jesus, in whom Baptists believe the practice of baptism originates, and texts from Paul, in whom Baptists believe the symbolic nature of baptism is most clearly understood. While other denominations may connect baptism to Old Testament cleansing rituals, most Baptists are reluctant to do so.

Also, the first point of Olson's sermon is "submerged" and the last point is "sanctification." What might that ordering imply? Many Baptists regard baptism by full immersion as the most— if not the only—efficacious means of administering the ordinance. This is why many Baptist congregations today require baptism by immersion for membership in the local church. Like Olson, they would use Scripture passages to support this requirement.

Finally, each of Olson's points about baptism is intended to point to what the individual does, or what happens to the individual as a result of baptism. Olson's approach implies that his sermon might have been intended to instruct new converts, but also implies that the main actor in the baptism event is the believer, not God. The believer is submerged under water, submits to Christ, symbolizes the death of Christ, serves the church, and becomes a representative of Christ's atonement. The individual nature of baptism is further emphasized in Olson's concluding point that baptism is a "private" bath. The Trinitarian reference at the end of the outline likely refers to a common phrase used by ministers at the baptism rite: "I baptize you in the name of the Father, the Son, and the Holy Ghost."

Introduction: Explain [Baptists'] historical relationship to Anabaptists. Baptism means:

1. Submerged. John 3:23; Acts 8:38–39; Matthew 3:16.
2. Submission (Obedience to [Christ's] command). Matthew 3:14–15; 28:19; Mark 16:15.
3. Symbolic (Buried, not sacramental). Colossians 2:12; Romans 6:3–5.
4. Service (Doorway to participation in church). Romans 12:1; Colossians 3:1–3.
5. Sanctification (Represents a cleansing from sin). Romans 6:6.
   Conclusion: "A private bath in the Name of the Trinity." (Cleansing and washing.)

The sermon outlines replicated here reflect their original formats.

Source: Used and replicated by permission of Ronald Olson.

Outline of Ronald Olson's Sermon on Christmas

In contrast to his sermons on baptism and the Lord's Supper, Olson's Christmas sermon reflects a different purpose and tone. Rather than mainly emphasize teaching of doctrine, this Christmas sermon seeks to evoke wonder and awe at the person of Jesus Christ based on the well-known prophecy of his birth from Isaiah 9:6. In his telling of Christ's significance, Olson never strays far from the question of the listener's personal relationship with the Savior.

NAMING THE BABY

Isaiah 9:6

Introduction: Months before our children were born, we already had names picked out, whether for a boy or for a girl. The name of the Son of God was chosen 710 years before Jesus was born. Isaiah wrote at that time: "And his name will be called . . ." Of course, what Isaiah gives us are traits of Christ as a person.

I. WONDERFUL or marvelous: Is Jesus Christ wonderful to you?
1. He was wonderful for leaving his throne. "To us a Son is given" . . . [this] means

Both this question and the songs quoted above are very direct. Whether in song or in sermon, the Baptists spent much time asking people to think about their personal relationship to Christ.

that when Jesus was born he had already lived from eternity. Many think that the Angel of Jehovah often mentioned in the Old Testament refers to Christ before his birth, or pre-incarnate.

Note the use of songs in this sermon. What dimension does the use of poetic material like songs bring to a sermon?

[Hymn or gospel song:]
Wonderful is Jesus, and so full of love,
Wonderful is Jesus, my Lord.
His name is matchless
I always want to praise him
Wonderful is Jesus, my Lord.

This was a stumbling block to the Jews . . . that Jesus Christ claimed to be divine and eternal, that he made himself equal to God.
Matthew 2:6, 7; Micah 5:2–4

2. He was wonderful in his humility.

To us a child is born. Genesis 3:15

[Song or chorus:]
How wonderful that Christ came down from heaven.
How wonderful that Christ died for me.
How wonderful that Christ is in heaven.
How wonderful that Christ is my mediator.

II. COUNSELOR Matthew 11:28
   Is Jesus Christ your Counselor?

   3. The counseling of Eve by the devil
   4. The counsel of the world. Psalm 1:1 and Proverbs 1:10
      My son, if sinners entice you, do not give in to them.
   5. The counsel of one's parents. Proverbs 1–7
   6. The counsel of friends
   7. The counsel of Christ . . .
      . . . to the sinner. Isaiah 1:18; 55:6
      . . . to the anxious. 1 Peter 5:7
      . . . to the believer. Matthew 6:33
      . . . to the weary. Matthew 11:28

III. MIGHTY GOD

"As man . . . as God" quote from Morrinson, *Decision*, Dec. '71, p. 8, "The Christ of the Gospel"

8. Philippians 4:13; Matthew 28:18–20

Our unbelief limits the power.

In the name of the Father, the Son, and the Holy Spirit

And surely I am with you always until the very end of the age. Amen. (Matthew 28:20)

IV. EVERLASTING FATHER

It is Christ who teaches us to pray, "Our Father who art in heaven . . ." God was not known as Father in the Old Testament.

V. PRINCE OF PEACE

9. Glory to God in the highest and on earth peace, good will to men. Luke 2:14.

10. Peace I leave with you; my peace I give you. I do not give to you as the world gives. Do not let your hearts be troubled and do not be afraid. John 14:27.

Peace with God, I sought to earn it, etc. [poem/hymn]

Is Christ all this for us?

Isaiah 53:5 and Romans 5:1

Source: Used and replicated by permission of Ronald Olson.

THEOLOGY OF WORSHIP DOCUMENTS

Ronald Olson's Instruction on the Nature of the Church

The following outline represents one sort of Bible study that Ronald Olson would have conducted with Ledesma Baptists. In it he seeks to provide a scriptural understanding of the church. Notice the lack of reference to clergy or the importance of Peter. Both omissions would have been noticed by former Roman Catholics in the mid-twentieth century. Of central concern in the lesson is the relationship of the worldwide or universal church to a local congregation. This doctrine of the church does not insist upon uniformity, liturgical or otherwise, as an important characteristic of the church. Again, this would contrast with 1950s-era Catholicism.

THE CHURCH OF JESUS CHRIST

Lesson 3

The formatting presented here represents the formatting of the original outline.

REVIEW:

Lesson 1

What the church is not: club, dogma, rules, politics, entertainment

What the church is:

You are the church.	*A divine body.*
	Christ = head.
1 Corinthians 12:27	Believer = member of the body.
Ephesians 5:30	If the foot has no part with the hand . . .
	If one suffers hemorrhage—veins shrink; it causes thirst.

Lesson 2: The Church, Universal and Local

The church is one. One body.

Christ prays for unity. John 17:21

—not for powers, hierarchies, super organizations

—for a spiritual oneness of faith, of purpose.

   I. United in *doctrine*: "one in mind" 1 Corinthians 1:10

  II. United in *discipline*: "one in thought," that is, in norms of conduct

 III. United in leading or developing *direction*: We believe in the unity of faith, not in union nor in uniformity. Not in minor details: hymnals, meeting times, etc.

Causes of different sects:

    1. Doctrinal

    2. Customs

    3. Geography

    4. History

    5. Race or nationality

    6. Disputes or strong leaders

Lesson 3

The use of the word church and what it means:

   I. Christ mentions the church only twice

Matthew 16:18 I will build my church. (Not on you, Peter.)

Matthew 18:17 Tell the church . . .

He speaks of the embryonic church.

The word in our Bible has its origin in the Greek language. It has two parts:

Ek   "outside of"

Klesia "called, removed, separate"

For the Greeks it meant an assembly of citizens, summoned to leave their homes and workplaces to meet and consider matters of public interest. Each man had the right to express his opinion and vote.

Jesus and his apostles adopted the word *ekklesia* to designate an assembly or congregation of Christ's followers, assembled and organized for the celebration of worship or for public service, and they gave it a deeper and more spiritual meaning.

  II. Christ and the apostles use the word church in two ways.

    1. The universal and ideal sense.

A broad sense embracing all saved persons in the whole world from the time of Jesus Christ and the first church which began on Pentecost to this moment

2. It is a divine, invisible, heavenly organism (something living)

Hebrews 12:33; Ephesians 5:24–29; 1 Corinthians 15:9

An organism is the totality of living parts of a living being, whether animal or plant. It is called the church triumphant. Hebrews 12:23 Perfect

This emphasis upon a visible, local church was critical.

3. A human, visible, earthly organization

This universal church is visibly made manifest in local churches, geographical[ly situated] in each town and place. In its local form it has a visible, human organization, temporal and without perfection. The local church signifies the entire group of saved persons, baptized by immersion, that meet in a designated place.

The Guerrero River is like the church universal, in the midst of the mountains of Jujuy—ancient, but not eternal. The water rushes along—from where does it come? Where is it going? For how long has it been running? The drops change, [but] the river remains. At times [it is] cloudy, dirty, full of mud. At times [it is] crystal clear, placid, transparent, tranquil, slow.

Notice the implicit message: it is close reading of the Bible that will give us the right form for truly being Christian.

4. In the New Testament

86 times it speaks of local churches

12 times it speaks of the church universal

Universal	Local
Ephesians 1:22–23	Matthew 18:17
Matthew 16:18	Revelation 2:7; 1:4, 11
1 Corinthians 15:5	1 Corinthians 5:13; 15:4
Galatians 1:13	Colossians 4:16
Colossians 1:24	Philippians 4:15
Hebrews 12:23	1 Corinthians 1:2
	Galatians 1:2
	Romans 16:5

The universal church is always manifested in a local, visible, earthly, human, imperfect church.

5. There are those who undervalue the idea of organization and a development plan in the local church and give all of the emphasis to the church universal. They oppose any organizational plan. They want everything to be informal and leave everything to the whim of the moment while saying that they are guided by the Holy Spirit.

Lesson 4

[The early church] [Originally this was part of lesson 3, but it has been bracketed by hand with instructions to add it to lesson 4, the theme of which is not stated here.]

Early local churches had:

1. Designated places of meeting

       The upper room   Acts 1:13

       The Temple   Acts 5:12

       The synagogues   Acts 12:12

       Houses   Acts 2:46

2. Defined meeting times   Acts 20:7; Hebrews 10:25

3. They counted those in attendance

    Acts 1:15   120 present

       2:41   3,000

        4:4   5,000

       2:47   a daily increase

4. They had office bearers and elections

    Philippians 1:1; Acts 1:23–26; 6:5–6; 20:17–18

    With authority   1 Peter 5:2

5. Letters of recommendation   Acts 18:27

6. A list of widows and needy   1 Timothy 5:9; Acts 6:1

7. Order in the meeting   1 Corinthians 14:40; Colossians 2:5

Source: Used by permission.

POLITY DOCUMENTS

Internal Document by Missionary Society Emphasizing Commitment to Cultivating Culturally Appropriate Churches

Try to read this document objectively. In what ways does it reflect an American ethnocentrism?

The following is a policy statement generated within the Conservative Baptist Foreign Mission Society in the 1950s to clarify the desire that its missionary activities create self-sustaining, indigenous churches rather than those dependent upon the foreign missionaries and out-of-country resources. Although the statement contains little direct reference to worship practices, its general sentiment would imply an openness to culturally developed, local worship. The document also makes clear the commitment to personal evangelism as the heart of the society's mission.

A Study of Indigenous Policies and Procedures

Prepared by the Foreign Department as a basis of discussion
by the Board of the Conservative Baptist Foreign Mission Society
April 17, 1952
Revisions made 1/5/53

Contents

The page numbers listed here refer to the original publication of the document.

I. The Indigenous Method Explained

Notice the first thing said in the statement and its implicit message: the proper guide for missions—as for all of Christianity—is the Bible.

Conservative Baptists are interested in the New Testament method for missions. If upon an examination of the New Testament method we find that it is indigenous, then we should apply indigenous methods to our mission work. We believe that the New Testament method as explained in Acts and through the Pauline epistles is indigenous.

A dictionary definition of indigenous reads as follows: "Originating in a specified place or country; not exotic; native; hence figuratively inherent." This definition will initiate our thinking, but it does not adequately present what is included in the word "indigenous" in the problem of foreign missions.

The same evangelizing zeal that brought the missionaries originally is to be built into the ethos of all the new Baptists and their congregations.

To be indigenous is neither the purpose nor the object of our work. The basic purpose of our work as a Foreign Mission Society is to send forth missionaries as ambassadors of Christ to proclaim a wonderful Savior, to teach the truths of an inspired Book, and to establish and expand New Testament churches in accordance with Christ's command. We cannot consider any task of evangelization well done that does not have as its goal the establishment of the new believers in the faith and in churches for the purpose of "reproducing" themselves. To achieve this God-given purpose we are attempting to follow God-given methods as they are set forth in the New Testament. We find this to be the indigenous method.

The words "self-supporting," "self-governing," and "self-propagating" are basic factors of the indigenous method. We will now examine these words remembering that no missionary work is fully indigenous unless all three factors are included.

A. Self-Supporting

The term "self-supporting" means exactly what it says. The financial needs of the church are met by the church members. Foreign funds are not a part of the church's financial picture. If foreign funds are used to support the pastor or factors of the church such as lighting, hymn books, janitor service, upkeep of the building, etc., then the full aspect of the financial approach is not self-supporting. In fact, we should start with the building itself. In order that a church can call itself self-supporting, it must erect its own building from the resources of the local church membership. We admit that there is a question which cannot be decided categorically as to whether or not a church is self-supporting when it accepts funds outside its own membership. There are some who feel it is quite right for neighboring church groups or any local element such as foreigners who earn their living by work such as a plantation or store or business within the country where the church is being developed to contribute financially. This is for all practical purposes still within the limits of self-support. To illustrate this concept in America, we expect a parent church to help a small mission church in the same city or in the country until that mission church gets on its feet. We would also not object to non-church members in the community such as business men contributing to the erection of the church building. In the same way, we may expect that a local church on the foreign field may look to any element within its own environment to help in its work. If such help is forthcoming we should not condemn the procedure as non-indigenous. All resources, therefore, whether from a local church membership or from elements of the surrounding environment are legitimate sources for the self-support of any local church.

Self-support includes more than money. Self-support includes also energy from human endeavor; that is, the activities of the church such as the choir and the Sunday School should be entirely from the local resources. It is true that some of these factors may overlap the self-governing of the church, but where we look upon these factors as units of energy, we realize that they form a part of the support of the church. This support should be from within itself and not from foreign sources. It is very likely that during the initial months and years of the mission church, the foreign missionaries may provide a great deal of this type of energy such as the development of the choir, the teaching of the Sunday School and the teaching in the formal services of the church. The sooner the missionary can turn these features over to individuals in the church, the sooner we can claim that the church is fully self-supporting.

The policy that newly planted churches were to be self-supporting meant that worship spaces would be simple and straightforward, often built by the members' own hands.

Notice the presumption for music-making. Would this section be different if it was written today? What contemporary forms and structures would need to be mentioned today?

B. Self-Government

This perhaps is one of the most difficult phases in the indigenous program of the church. The temptation and habit of the missionary to carry on certain features of the government of the church is almost irresistible. Is the missionary not the father of the church? Did he not bring it into being, as it were, with the help of the Holy Spirit and God? Therefore, the various items related to the government of the church from the very start have been indicated by the wisdom of the missionary. It is difficult for the nationals to carry on the work of the church independent of the missionary. They have from the start depended on his wisdom and they continue to do so as the church grows. It is only the energy of the Holy Spirit coupled with resistance within the soul of the missionary that will turn over all the factors involved in the government of the church—all its committees, its treasureship, trusteeship, its discipline, its preaching and teaching functions to the nationals. All of it must be by the local members. This can probably best be achieved as the missionary takes the time to turn to the Bible, when problems arise, and show the nationals what God's Word has to say. In this way, the nationals will learn that it is the Bible and not the missionary which is indispensable. Thus, the factor of self-government will become effective in the indigenous program.

C. Self-Propagating

The evangelistic impulse is clearly evident here. It would be an expected part of the church's ongoing life and worship, even as the leadership became more national. One can sense here the motivation to prepare new converts for evangelistic leadership.

We all recognize that the factor of self-propagation is most important. No church will live long unless it propagates itself. In fact, it is not a Christian church if generation by generation it does not re-propagate itself in the hearts and lives of human beings. For some missionaries the imparting of this procedure is a definite gift given from God. The first converts are hardly over their first testimony of God's grace in their hearts before they have been instructed and encouraged and sent out to win others, to propagate themselves. Other missionaries do not seem to have this gift and although they themselves are able to evangelize and build a sizeable church, molding the Christians together in a unit, they do not impart to these Christians this primary purpose for every Christian—namely, the spreading of the Gospel into the hearts and lives of other men and women. The Lord Jesus sent forth His disciples with this definite purpose. They went out to tell others of salvation. It is obvious that at the start of any missionary work where there are no Christians, the missionary must be the one to win the heathen to Christ. As soon as a group has been won and a church has started, the missionary must expect that the winning of souls and the building up of souls which is a part of the self-propagation must be the function of the local Christians. If this is not so, he should review his work and his teaching ministry to see what is the lack and cause of this failure. Perhaps there is a lack of prayer.

The teaching ministry has a bearing on the self-propagation of the church. Self-propagation does not mean merely souls who accept the Lord Jesus. It means that they must become established in their own individual growth and in the growth of the group as a local church until they stand firm in the Lord. Soon after Christian groups are started, this teaching ministry can become a partial function of the local Christians. The missionary need not be the only source of teaching. In fact, all the functions of the missionary should eventually be taken over by the local church. So long as a missionary is allowed to remain in a given environment, he will naturally try to win souls and to build up souls in Christ, but the church should be so organized or grouped that these three functions—that of self-support, self-government, and self-propagation—shall be the mature and certain characteristics of the church.

II. Why Indigenous Methods in Their Full Implications Are Not Stressed by Many Mission Boards

Our problems and differences of opinion have arisen, not in determining the purpose of our work but in trying to decide which methods are most Scriptural in achieving lasting results. We are trying to discover how far materials and methods foreign to the culture in which we are working can be used without hindering the establishment of New Testament churches in that land. Admittedly, the problem is not one which has an easy solution. The very fact that many Mission Boards do not stress the indigenous method with all of its implications in either their approach on the mission field or in their teaching material at home, indicates that it is not a popular method. Let us briefly examine why this is so.

A. It Produces Results Slowly

America is noted around the world for its business "know how," its ability to "get things done," its efficiency. As Americans we chafe under delays and are constantly looking for ways to "finish the job" we have set out to do. Within the boundaries of our evangelical standards, anything that will produce results more rapidly is looked upon with favor even though the permanent results may not be as satisfactory as other methods that might be used. In America where the church has been established, we can turn hundreds of converts over to the old church, but in many foreign lands new converts have no churches to attend and the function of a missionary in addition to being a personal soul-winner, is to be a church-planter. This is usually a slow, glamorless job which goes against the grain of our modern, efficient American way of doing things.

Probably what is in mind here are large-scale evangelistic meetings, where many make decisions for Christ. Imagine a Billy Graham crusade.

B. It Is Discouraging

Anyone who has tried to establish a church in America knows how discouraging such work can be. Only a small nucleus is available to start the work, the offerings are small, personality problems arise, a faithful one of the small band dies, [and] new folk do not seem to be attracted. The work of an evangelist seems to be much easier where the discouragements of the local church problems will not have to be faced. These same discouragements can more afflict the missionary and he cries out in his frustration, "If only I could have more money from home to build a church, to build a school where more nationals could be trained, to have a larger hospital or dispensary where more needs could be met and to hire more workers." Activity is many times used by Satan as a counterfeit of results. Discouragement at the apparent lack of results is a strong deterrent to the indigenous method.

C. It Curtails Promotion at Home

By this phrase we do not mean that it curtails the promoting of our task as Christians to get the Gospel into all the world. It does, however, curtail the promoting of many financial projects which evangelical Christians have taken for granted in any missionary program in past years. These projects have included the support of an orphan, paying for a student's training, salary of a native worker, etc. Mission Boards have tried to meet the demand of constituencies for projects which can be undertaken by individuals who cannot give large amounts of money and as a result many of these smaller projects have developed. A strictly indigenous method would rule out most of these.

The slow process of church-planting along indigenous lines also makes it frequently impossible to thrill the churches with glowing reports from the fields. In these days of high-pressure advertising, even our Christian people may measure success by numbers. Knowing this, the missionary is sorely tempted to yield to the known attitudes of the folk at home and to use methods that will produce large though superficial results.

This study makes repeated references to mid-century American society and its cultural influences. Does this document take into account the subtle values American-born missionaries might take with them?

D. It Apparently Contradicts the Christian Message of Helping Those Less Fortunate Than Ourselves

In addition to the above reasons as to why indigenous methods are not too popular, there is one that is even more basic; namely, should not we, as Christians, help those who are less fortunate? With our knowledge of medicines, agriculture, hygiene, etc., and with our high standard of living, should we not help in a material way those who are in need, even starving to death and dying because of a lack of medicine? Does not the Bible say "Suppose some brother or sister is ill-clad and short of daily food; if any of you tell them, 'depart in peace! Get warm, get food,' without supplying their bodily needs, what use is that? So faith, unless it has deeds, it is dead in itself." (James 2:15–17, Moffatt) Where do the social implications of the Gospel come in? Where and when do the by-products of the Gospel (good works) reveal themselves? This is one of the most basic problems to answer as we attempt to determine where our indigenous methods should be applied. Perhaps, for sake of clarification, this can be discussed under several headings.

1. If we were speaking of conditions within our own forty-eight states, this question would be much easier to answer. Someone immediately says, "Why? What is the difference between helping those in need in our land and those in need in another?" The core of the answer is possibly found in this statement—"Though all Christians are members of that 'one body in Christ,' we still live in a world of various cultures and environments." As long as we live in a sinful world, these cultures and environments will have their effects in our relationships to each other upon all but the most consecrated Christians. We do not realize this so much because we are in America, the symbol of plenty where prosperity abounds, and thus it is hard to imagine the feelings which those living in less fortunate lands have toward "rich America." As we impose our "more cultured" ways and "better methods" on other peoples, we do not realize how the culture and nationalistic feeling of that land rises up in protest—not because we are trying to help them but because we infer that their way is inferior to our way. It is exactly this point which Communism uses as a fulcrum to pry countries away from the western powers. By exploiting the natural and more basic urge for freedom and self-government, Russia has blinded the eyes of many national leaders to other benefits our Western civilization has introduced. The problem has been put this way, "He (the missionary) is called to cross national and cultural barriers which separate the peoples of this world. He is the 'apostle to the Gentiles,' a calling which necessitates a break with his own people and the adoption of a new home in a strange land. But the mere fact that a person leaves his native land for a foreign shore is no indication that the national or cultural barrier has been crossed. The missionary frequently fails to make the break. He takes America with him. He establishes a small colony within the walls of the mission compound. . . . No effort is made to adopt the ways of the foreign country as we would expect a guest to adjust his life in the home of a friend."

2. We must always realize why we are in a foreign land—to establish the Church of Christ. The reason we are so interested in missions is not only because Christ has commanded us to "go into all the world," but because we have realized the value of a soul. We know it does *not* profit if a man gains the whole world and loses his own soul. For this reason we are interested in evangelism—in getting people to accept God's gift of salvation through Jesus Christ. When,

Some missiological studies of the mid-twentieth century would note this tendency as a reason why this missionary approach sometimes produced sparse results. As a general principle, rejection of this isolating tendency would spread as a critique of many American churches in the late twentieth century. Have you ever heard of a congregation being faulted for being only concerned for itself, putting up barriers of language and music to make it hard for the outsider to feel at home?

By placing in quotation marks the phrases "more cultured" and "better methods," the document is trying to project objectivity on a propensity for cultural bias. The quotation marks indicate the relativity of American ways. But consider how easily it is to ignore those quotation marks, creating a presumption of American rightness, even by the "most consecrated Christians."

through the Holy Spirit's leadership, this is accomplished, it not only gives peace in the midst of existing conditions, but usually gives an individual a desire to apply himself to better his social conditions. In securing the social benefits of the Gospel, it would seem that those who hold to indigenous principles are as much in favor of them as any other Christian group with a modification that the supporters of indigenous work believe these benefits, the care of the widows and orphans, the healing of the sick, the education and training of the Christian constituency, should come through the church instead of through the missionary. Initial organizational plans and leadership may come from the missionary but ideally the material support should come from the local church environment. This is the indigenous method, the New Testament way. To allow foreign material resources to underwrite these features of the local church program is to weaken the church. It will stunt its growth. If the foreign elements are removed from a church supported and upheld largely by foreign resources, the local church is liable to disintegrate because of the lack of internal strength. This would be like the new building that fell down when the scaffold was removed. The scaffold is only a temporary structure. So the activities of the missionary should be only temporary. When the missionary leaves, the church that remains should be strong and durable. Indeed this is a test for any missionary work. When the foreign elements are removed, does the work prove itself independent in its supporting, governing, and propagating aspects? Between those who can only think and work for social betterment in foreign lands and those whose missionary work is only for the salvation of souls, are those with the concept of saving souls in order that the national Christian church may be established which, in turn, will become the "salt" of the earth and implement the social blessings of the Christian church. Anything that is not assisting in establishing the Church of Christ should be discouraged. Anything that hinders the development of the Church, no matter how much immediate good it does, should be sacrificed for the slower but more permanent good achieved by the establishment of the indigenous church.

The study is rejecting an approach to missions that had developed among some denominations that emphasized caring for physical needs rather than personal evangelism.

3. Another fact that should be recognized in our thinking if we are to answer the question "why not 'clothe' and 'feed' our Christian brethren," is the impossibility of doing the job. At this point, in spite of appearing hard-hearted, we should remind ourselves of this inescapable fact—the nationals who are dying by the hundreds and thousands due to a lack of proper nourishment and medicine WERE DYING YEARS BEFORE WE CAME TO THE LAND! At best we can only reach a small proportion of the millions in need and the danger is that Satan will cause us to see the material needs and tempt us to dissipate our personnel and resources in alleviating these physical needs to the detriment of meeting the spiritual needs of these multitudes. It is better that a person die at 20 with Christ than at 75 without Him. The place of medical activity in missionary endeavor will be discussed later, but the point that is emphasized here is that the material needs of the under-privileged multitudes on our fields can never be fully met.

4. By assisting the nationals to better their conditions with American funds and plans, there is always the danger of confusing the minds of the people we are trying to reach as to what Christianity really is. In the minds of many of the national Christians, the Gospel message, with its emphasis on salvation, becomes mixed with the material by-products of the Gospel. These babes in Christ have not yet reached the place where they realize that what we are doing is in the name of Christ. They look upon the by-products which we introduce as the content of the Gospel, and, of course, they are glad to follow in the train of those who sponsor these material things. They have unknowingly joined the group who followed Jesus because they thought He would be King and provide them with food. They thought they would be healed from all of their physical trouble because their King was sufficient. So the national sees the great possibilities of American resources and feels that if he joins the Christian group, he too will be free from further troubles in matters of clothes, food and health. The "natural" man is so made that he gladly takes hold of a new "religion" which can apparently help his physical and material needs. We must constantly combat this "natural" feeling by presenting in word and deed the "spiritual" nature and eternal value of our message.

Is this conclusion a reasonable comparison to the Gospel stories of Jesus's ministry? See John 6.

5. The pursuance of social service activities by the missionary becomes a matter of substituting the better for the best. The purpose and task of a missionary is to win souls to Christ, to build up souls in Christ, and to plant churches. There is nothing wrong in social service in the name of Christ; it is the right thing for a Christian—the "works" of the Epistle of James. This should be the activity of the church which the missionary is planting—but not of the missionary himself. If the missionary does give his time and energy to this, he is substituting the better for the best.

6. Is there a place for social service by a missionary? Yes, as an individual but not as a missionary. As an individual the missionary will always be helping in social service activities, donating money from his personal funds, ministering to the sick, etc., but he should not as a missionary use mission funds. He will, as a Christian, administer the cup of cold water in Christ's name but as a missionary he will concentrate his energy, time and foreign resources on the main task of planting the church.

We may give a beggar a dollar as an individual but surely we cannot feed all the beggars in the world. The missionary's task is to get a redeemed people organized into a church which, if really saved and properly instructed, will have a social conscience toward their fellow-countrymen. In this way the principles taught by Jesus in Matthew 25:31–46 can be effectively fulfilled.

III. Modern Practices Which Complicate the Introduction of New Testament Methods in Missions

Notice the quotation marks around the word "Christian." This is a way of saying that the form of Roman Catholicism the document has in mind is not really apostolic and congruent with the New Testament. The attitude between the two groups was more competitive than cooperative.

There are many problems facing a Christian missionary today which were completely unknown in Paul's day. Competition from a so-called "Christian" church (Roman Catholic), modern transportation with its high original cost and continued upkeep, the many mission lands where illiteracy abounds, the great difference in standards of living, and denominational problems—none of these problems were faced by Paul. The Roman Catholic Church with its grandeur and pomp tempts the Christian missionary to attempt the building of a meeting place which will in a small way compete in attraction with a large church. Modern transportation and mechanical developments pose the problem as to how far we should go in introducing modern methods of transportation and time-saving implements. Can an indigenous church be established with illiterates? What shall we do about the great difference in the standard of living when compared with ours? How can the White Cross program be integrated into the indigenous approach? What about denominational problems which Paul did not face as we face them today? Let us consider each of these problems briefly and relate them to the indigenous approach.

A. The Roman Catholic Church and the Indigenous Method

The contrast is immediately seen. One stresses external things to attract and hold its people. The other stresses the internal condition of the soul. One is natural—the other is spiritual. Our battle is not carnal but spiritual. While there is no reason why a New Testament church should not work to have a neat and attractive meeting place, to feel that spending foreign funds for better places of worship is necessary in order to compete against an apostate hierarchy is completely to overlook the place of the Holy Spirit in our work.

Does the reverse hold true? Does worship for high-tech people need to be technologically sophisticated? That argument is often made to justify the ever-increasing technological complexity of "contemporary worship."

B. Modern Transportation and Mechanical Developments and the Indigenous Method

We go to the mission field primarily to save souls and establish New Testament churches. Will modern transportation and mechanical inventions help or hinder in this work? The answer will be determined somewhat by the area where the missionary is going to work. Of course, modern transportation should be used to take the missionary to and from his field. The problem arises when we reach the field and the station. How much should a mission car be in evidence? How does a P.A. system fit into the indigenous plan? What about power saws and electric lights? Here is one place where we enter into a highly debatable area of thinking and where both sides can be logical and still not agree. Indigenous methods, strictly applied, would rule out these modern factors if they were beyond the mechanical and technological level of the people we are trying to reach. If the nationals could not carry on with these modern things without the help of the white man and if they could not afford to buy them if they had to be replaced, then there is a doubt as to its advisability. It can just as logically be argued that the using of these modern things increases the effectiveness of the missionary a thousand percent. Both arguments are logical and right. This illustration may throw a bit of light on the problem—a good father can do a certain job much better and much faster than his son, but he lets the son do it in order to teach the son how to do it. He is preparing the son for the day when he will be on his own. He will not train the son with tools which the son himself cannot have later in life. From this illustration we may draw the general conclusion which may answer both logical arguments expressed above—as far as possible on compounds and stations the missionary should use the transportation and mechanical developments used by the people. This is one phase of "reaching them on their own level."

Writing in Life Magazine, Mr. Charles Malik, Lebanon minister to the United Nations Assembly said, "The West must be tolerant of economic methods alien to its own habits. . . . Technological efficiency cannot be grafted upon a culture from the outside."

Where the missionary, after prayer and consideration, feels that the advantages gained by using modern things more than offset the disadvantages, he should use them only for personal use and not try to integrate them into the indigenous church. (Illustration—use a saw mill and a truck to build but do not give the saw and truck to the national church.) In an effort to remove the thought that the missionary is wealthy, he should explain to the nationals that the money for these things [is] sacrificially given by people in America, in order that more people might hear the Gospel than would otherwise be possible. Through all of this it should be kept in mind that spiritual concepts taught are far more important and lasting than any material progress made. Reaching the minds and hearts of the people because they feel you are one of them is of more importance and produces more lasting results than trying to speed up material processes. Even though the nationals may greatly desire the foreign aid, we must carefully evaluate whether or not it will weaken the recipients.

C. Illiteracy and the Indigenous Method

Here we meet a more serious difference between Paul's day and ours. Paul's contacts were in areas of literacy, particularly in Greece and Rome. In many lands today, however, missionary work begins and functions among an illiterate group. In order to bring this illiterate group to the place of understanding and ability to read the New Testament, we must develop a definite

Note how the reference to "the white man" introduces, in typical mid-twentieth-century fashion, race and gender into the discussion about the discrepancy of initial resources.

literacy campaign. Paul did not have to do this. His people could read and write and were able to use any literature and letters which were circulated among them. Any program which attempts to raise the literacy rate of the people involves a program of education. Remembering the Scripture, "Faith cometh by hearing and hearing by the Word of God," and remembering that we are to "teach them (new Christians) all things whatsoever I have commanded you," it seems impossible that an indigenous church could be established among the illiterates. They can be Christians, yes—but not a self-governing church. In some of our lands (Japan, Italy, Portugal) we are working among people who can read. In others the missionary has to become the teacher. In Congo the government has made the whole problem of education a responsibility of the mission. If we start subsidized educational work, where do we stop?

Here again let us think in terms of a New Testament church. A missionary arrives and begins to witness. The Holy Spirit works in the hearts of the nationals and souls are saved. Immediately a teaching program must be initiated. In addition to giving them the "milk of the Word," classes in reading must be started and if Bible portions are not already translated into the native language, translation work should begin in order that the Bible may become the textbook for teaching the rudiments of reading. In an area like the Kivu where the government is making us responsible for the education of our Christian constituency, we have been forced to open schools. In other lands the method may be that of the Laubach system or the communistic-trained few who will go out and teach others. As a mission society, it would seem that we should train pastors who will go to villages and become the spiritual and educational leaders of the community even as the pastors were in the early days in New England. In other words, the educational program is primarily to assist in establishing the indigenous church. In accordance with II Tim. 2:2 we are to teach them in order that they may go out and reach their own people. Surely there is a place for educational work in the process of establishing the indigenous church. The problem in connection with educational work is—how much material help should be sent from America? Where we furnish more than the missionary (in Congo we now have to do more), to that extent we are in danger of causing the national church to lean on foreign help instead of encouraging them to take the initiative wholly themselves. "Pump-priming" may be necessary in some cases but every effort should be made to encourage the church to take part of the initiative and responsibility. When we hold back from giving material aid, it is not because we do not wish to assist our brothers and sisters in Christ, but rather we do not wish to encourage them to lean on America beyond what is absolutely necessary and we do not wish prematurely to introduce methods and materials that will hinder the national Christians in winning their fellow-countrymen to Christ.

Is it ironic that a "conservative" mission society is emphasizing radical notions of literacy that have often led to new, indigenous forms of Christianity and, more broadly, democratic political sensibilities? Andrew Walls summarizes this dynamic in Akintunde Akinade, ed., *A New Day: Essays on World Christianity in Honor of Lamin Sanneh:* (1) missionary movements adopt the local vernacular languages, with translation of the Scriptures as an early aim; (2) vernacular Bible translation releases a force for indigenous cultural liberation and renewal; (3) this force opens the way for indigenous creative innovation, thought, expression, and even music.

D. *Difference in Standard of Living*

It is a recognized fact that there is a great contrast between the standard of living in the United States and most countries where foreign missionaries now work. The standards in the United States and Europe are vastly different from those found in Asia, South America, and Africa. There is, therefore, the unconscious temptation on the part of the missionary to feel that he should try to raise the standard of living of the people to whom he ministers. The standard of living which he considers the norm is, of course, that of the United States of America.

This is a false premise. Christian salvation is not a matter of civilization. It is true that backward civilizations have been greatly improved by the influence of the Lord Jesus Christ in the hearts and lives of His followers but this is a by-product of Christianity and is a historical result whenever Christ becomes an influence in the hearts of individuals. This change in the standard of living, however, should come *through the national church* and not be imposed by foreign missionaries. Ideally, the only time financial assistance for an improved standard of living should be given to the Christian in foreign lands is when the standard has been lowered *below the normal standard* for that area by unusual circumstances—such as flood, famine, etc.

The Gospel of salvation is effective in changing any people on any level of civilization. The duty of the missionary is not primarily to introduce higher standards of living. The duty and task of the missionary is to preach the Gospel and assist in building the church. The raising of the standard of living will take care of itself. Satan is very eager to throw a smoke-screen or fog around the whole missionary process in an effort to get the missionary and the new Christians to dissipate their energies in an effort to change the physical aspects found in the mode of living. When we depart from the New Testament procedure we are indeed apt to fall by the wayside of secular pursuits related to the standard of living.

Perhaps there is nothing more tempting to violate indigenous methods than in the medical phase of our work. Having been trained in our modern, sanitary hospitals with all equipment available and having been taught the value of physical life, it is only natural that the missionaries as well as the doctors should carry this American concept of medical work to the field and attempt to reproduce it. He sees the great need and knowing what American medicine can do, his vision is able to involve him in thousands of dollars for medicine, equipment and buildings. This insistence upon high medical standards of treatment for the nationals requires subsidization from foreign funds as the standard of living found on the field is unable to support the level of medical treatment we are used to in America. Where should the fulfillment of this vision be limited? The answer can best be found in seeking before God how this program can be set up so that eventually it will be carried on by trained national Christians. At the same time it should be remembered that medicine is a God-given means to the primary end of saving souls for eternity. There should be a training program initiated which will make it possible for the nationals to do simple diagnosis and to dispense simple remedies for the same. Although we desire high standards for our medical missionaries, we cannot expect the same thing throughout the church organization as this is at first too elaborate for them to support, and involves a subsidization on the part of the missionary organization which disturbs the effort to establish an indigenous church. It may also tie up money which could be used to send out additional missionary personnel. It has been shown in areas like the Lisu work in the China Inland Mission that this whole situation can take care of itself as a by-product of missionary work if the missionary and the Christians will concentrate upon the winning of souls and the building up of the church.

Serious consideration should be given to the personal position of the American missionary. Because of our own standard of living it is natural that we bring many material things which are in great contrast to the civilization where we go. Even a minimum of equipment is in contrast to what the people of that land have. The missionary, therefore, faces a personal problem of how he can integrate his own personal belongings so that they will not be barriers and hindrances in his presentation of the wonderful Gospel of Jesus Christ, the Savior of men. It is unwise for us to set down specific standards and definite lists of what equipment to take and what not to take. When the missionary becomes cognizant of his problem, the Holy Spirit will guide him to do that which will enable the Holy Spirit to work effectively through him to accomplish his main job of building the church.

E. White Cross and the Indigenous Method

The White Cross was a Christian humanitarian organization originally formed by two Baptist women in Ohio. Many American congregations participated.

White Cross originally developed in order to help hospitals and medical work. Whether it was a doctor or nurse or the general missionary, the supplies sent from home such as bandages and other related materials used for the hospital and in dispensary work as well as out in the villages for open clinics, were a great asset in the lands where such things are not available. As the activities of the women in the home churches increased, they branched out into assisting any needy part of the missionaries' contacts. Schools where pencils and paper were not available at reasonable prices were helped by the contributions from the White Cross churches in America. Christmas provided a logical time when gifts for Sunday School scholars and Christians could naturally be given. This was, of course, in the period when much was made of Christmas and the thought of "white Christmas" had not developed on the foreign fields. Thus it became a regular custom for the home churches to send boxes with Christmas gifts for the missionaries. The missionaries, of course, were unselfish and pleaded for gifts for the children and then later for the Christians themselves, until the possibilities were expanded extensively beyond the original medical supply.

Perhaps the last stage of White Cross activities is found in the old clothes gathered by the church people and sent to the missionary. This was greatly emphasized as war relief particularly after the last two wars. It was only natural when the acute war condition ended that these same efforts should be extended to foreign fields where poverty always existed. These clothes, therefore, became the object of missionaries' help for school children and for needy people, particularly the Christians, in any field.

Many years of experience in this have given us a basis whereby we can analyze the results of the White Cross upon the people themselves. It is quite apparent that whether it is in Africa, South America or in Asia the people react much the same. They begin to expect this help wherever and whenever they can. In time, if one missionary has been dealing extensively in this sort of thing and a new missionary comes who does not have the resources of the old missionary, it becomes a serious basis of comparison between the old and the new. Obviously the mission should try to evaluate the results as to whether or not this fits into the indigenous program; that is, the sound building of a church group.

We have a basis for evaluation when we take the New Testament as our norm for the growth of the church. When we analyze the psychological results of free drugs, free schooling and free supplies upon the Christians, we soon find what is called the "Rice Christian" psychology manifesting itself. The people, being very human, naturally gravitate to where they can receive these material helps and when the material help is not forthcoming, then the individual missionary begins to sense a definite loss of interest in his services. Some of these people being very primitive are very frank and remark, "What is the use of being a Christian if we do not receive these benefits?" Then it is that we begin to realize that these things which we thought were to help the people have only hindered and confused them. The Gospel message and its intent has become mixed up with the benefits which we thought were so essential as an outward expression of our concept of the Gospel. These babes in Christ have not yet reached the place where they realize what we are doing is in the name of Christ. They think it is *the* message and, of course, they are glad to follow in the train of those who deal out these materials. They have unconsciously joined the group who followed Jesus because they thought He would be King and provide them with food. They thought they would be healed, they would have no more physical problems, their King was sufficient. So the simple national sees the large amount of American resources and feels that if he joins in that group, he too will be free from further troubles in matters of clothing and food and health.

Eventually a clear-thinking missionary begins to realize that these benefits must be foregone if he is to get the true message of salvation and Jesus' purpose in coming to this world across to these people who have lived in heathen darkness and idolatrous practices.

Some think, and probably correctly, that there is still a place for the medical needs from White Cross. Certain situations in certain fields require school supplies. Books may well be supplied through White Cross as from grants and donations from the mission itself. Beyond this, there is real doubt whether missionaries should engage in the traffic of old clothes and other things for normal Christians. The Christian constituency will do better in its spiritual growth if it is not confused by the introduction of Western resources and products.

Let us go back to the New Testament and seeking the example of Paul in the organization and founding of his churches discover those principles which will guide us and apply them directly to our White Cross program.

F. Denominational and Mission Board Problems

Paul did not represent a definite denomination. Neither was he sponsored by a mission board. He was commissioned and sent out by the church, [and] after that the Holy Spirit directed his travels and sponsored his physical well-being. In the normal development of Christendom and what we believe is by the direct guiding of the Holy Spirit, the Church has developed until we have many denominations and each denomination usually has a foreign mission board which sponsors the activity of its missionaries.

The missionary today, therefore, is guided a great deal through the Board of his denomination. His theology is in accord with his particular denomination.

These direct influences have a tendency to keep the missionary from following clearly and definitely the pure New Testament procedures laid down by St. Paul and other writers in the New Testament.

The problem, therefore, of finding what is the true procedure, un-adulterated by our denominational emphases and our mission board standards, is a problem not only for the missionary but also for the Board to work out. Once we have conscientiously yielded our corporate organization as well as our individual selves to the guidance of the Holy Spirit and faced this situation we perhaps are in the way to find the leading of the Spirit and to establish our procedures and policies along the New Testament lines.

IV. The Importance of Using Indigenous Methods

Why should our Society be interested in conducting mission work along indigenous lines?

Not surprisingly, the reliance upon Scripture is the first reason stated.

A. We believe it is the Scriptural way

Paul launched his missionary work with the impetus of the inspiration received from the older church in Antioch which, in turn, received its start from the testimony given by

Christians from Jerusalem. As he went forth, however, he worked in terms of the village, city, country and people where he traveled. His greatest handicap came through the Jews who tried to impose upon the new churches certain regulations which the old churches were trying to follow. This matter had to be worked out back in Jerusalem with the older church. The result, however, was a victory for the new churches that they should be allowed to proceed according to the Holy Spirit's guidance. There was an agreement to follow certain policies of the old church which did not materially influence or affect the growth of the new churches.

The development of the new churches was always in terms of the Holy Spirit's action within the hearts of the new Christians. The elders and officers were selected from the local environment. *This means they had self-government.* Paul remained only a comparatively short time—just long enough to get the church started. After that it grew and developed in terms of its own initiative and the efforts of its own members. *This is self-propagation.* We cannot find anywhere in the New Testament that those early churches were subsidized by funds from the old churches. Always they took care of their own expenses. *This was self-support.* We do, of course, find the incidents where the new churches sent help back to the old church in Jerusalem. We do not advocate isolationism. We do know that fellowship is greatly to be desired between both old and new churches. If there is a need beyond the norm of the local environment in either place that can be filled by the other, the one church, of course, would follow the example of Christian teaching and help those in need. This, however, should not be a continuous need, but, as in all cases of the New Testament, a special circumstance which inspires the sharing of material help between the new and the old churches.

B. We believe it gives the Holy Spirit more freedom to work in the national churches

By following the New Testament method, there is freedom for the Holy Spirit to work in terms of the local environment which otherwise becomes curtailed. The occidental attitude toward all activity is to impose its own initiative and general organizational energy. Whereas this does add greatly to the rapid growth of an early group or organization whether it be a church or any other type of organization which the West may be interested in developing in foreign areas, the long range view is much different. We find that these foreign introductions usually tend to hinder the local initiative and to curtail the normal growth that would come by the impetus of the Holy Spirit within changed lives. These born-again Christians become confused as they try to adopt foreign methods. They are continually striving to satisfy the older, the more experienced and dominating foreign group. After the first five or ten years, the growth of the church becomes stagnant. Unless there is a definite and complete return to the indigenous approach, the church group itself is apt to die. An example of this is the

The reference is likely to church historian Kenneth Scott Latourette (1884-1968).

mission work in Paraguay where the Roman Catholic church carried on a paternal work for 100 years. When the European staff was withdrawn, the Christians apostasized and the missions declined (Latourette, Vol. III, pp. 154–56).

Why might Americans have been especially sensitive to this accusation in the 1950s?

C. We believe it is an answer to charges of "American imperialism"

Whether it is true or not, we must acknowledge that the Communists have slanted their propaganda in backward countries to cater to the rising tides of nationalism, which is such a dominant force in the world today. "American imperialism" is a charge that is constantly aimed by the Communists toward any kind of work which America is doing in other countries. In the January 1, 1952, issue of "The Farmer Lutheran Evangelist"—Chao Fei Wu, from Loyang in Honan, has an article entitled: "The Church of China Must Begin Anew." We cannot quote the article in full, but it is of value to note excerpts of his letter as written to the editors who have used it as a foreword to the article. His emphasis is on the idea that there must be a New Church of China built by the masses. That is the most important thing in these times, which must not be overlooked. He states that the Christians of China all hate denominational lines, regardless of what branch of the Christian faith it may be. He says: "The People's Church of China from today must have a new beginning—with one Name, one Hymnbook, and under one leadership. A part of the Church of China has a pure Faith. The former workers in the Church must accept the thinking of the Christian masses, and must lead the Christians against the use of the Church by the Imperialists—particularly the American Imperialists."

While it is true that this quotation is from a Communist, a perusal of current magazines and newspapers will reveal that in many quarters America is looked upon with suspicion because of its aggressive leadership and when the rising tide of nationalism fully engulfs some of the fields where our missionaries are now laboring, the above quotation will, in substance, be said of us to the extent that we have not been indigenous. Dr. Charles Malik, in his article "From a Friend of the West," said: "It is ironic that nationalism—one of the few political ideas successfully exported by the West to Asia—today is the source of so much of Asia's hostility to the West. . . . The notions of the city or the state (or the nation), in the modern sense, of the equality of all citizens within the state, of representative government and of the will of the people as the foundation of civil authority—all these came to Asia for the most part from the West. In diverse ways, these are the very ideas exploited by Communism to inflame anti-Western feeling.

"Europe has taught the world that no greater disgrace can befall one people than to be politically subject to another. This lesson Asia has learned with a vengeance. . . . The idea of one's nation, one's motherland, whose independence is to be attained and safeguarded at any price, [from] which 'the foreigner' must be driven by all means, has taken firm hold on the Asiatic imagination." In the April 9th edition of the Christian Science Monitor there appeared an article written by Robert Hollett, staff writer on Latin America affairs on Communistic influence in Brazil. In it he said, "Enemies call it Communist (one group in Brazil), but it ranges all the way from Communists and fellow travelers to extreme nationalists, who are lumped with the Communists only because of their bitter dislike of United States influence in Brazil." These typical quotations clearly reveal the importance of missionaries working along the line of indigenous procedures. The more we are able to put the responsibility of the national church onto the nationals themselves, to that extent we will avoid unnecessary criticism from the national leaders where we are working.

Some of our evangelical mission leaders in America warn us that the hour is late! They state that unless the Lord intervenes, we are living in the sunset of missionary work in many countries. While we do not wish to be pessimistic, we want to be realistic and the more we can get the national Christians to assume places of leadership in the national church while we are there to counsel with them, the better chance the national church will have to survive after the white missionaries have been forced to leave.

D. We believe it makes for a stronger national church

The experiences of one of our missionaries as she began a new church in the village of her residence will perhaps give us some ideas as to the actual working of the indigenous principles.

The first problem that faced her was a meeting place. The small handful of Christians naturally looked to the missionary's residence for it was perhaps more commodious than any of their homes. The missionary, however, said, "No." They must provide the place for themselves. This seemed rather harsh and unsympathetic, but it drove the Christians to become resourceful and to consider the solution of their problems without the benefit of the missionary and the missionary's resources. They found a place and therefore the transition from the missionary's home to another place was never necessary. Had they begun to meet in the home of the missionary, they would have been satisfied to stay there indefinitely. Today these Christians have not only rented their church building, but have begun to build their own place of worship.

The next problem was chairs for use during the service. No Christian had enough chairs in his home so they immediately turned to the missionary and asked if they could not borrow the missionary's chairs during the time of worship. Again the missionary said, "No." It did look as though the missionary was not willing to share but it was a problem for the church to find a solution and they did.

The next item that came up for consideration was a light for the evening meetings. They used very small lamps or wicks burning in dishes of oil. These lights, of course, are only good for a general breaking of the darkness in a room or for one individual to use in reading. Again they turned to the missionary for she had the only adequate light. The missionary gave in here and allowed them to use her light. Months passed; in fact a year passed. That missionary's remark is most enlightening—"And who provided oil for that lamp?" The missionary, of course. Did not the lamp belong to the missionary? Therefore the missionary must provide the oil. Thus we see that when the missionary finally did give in to share in the work and in the church development, this giving in was the entrance for the Christians to use something belonging to the missionary. So until the missionary left, the Christians used not only the lamp but the oil of the missionary.

Would you agree that this policy is wise?

These things may seem very small. One could condemn the missionary as heartless and indifferent for refusing to share with the simple needs of the Christians. If we investigate further, however, we realize the wisdom of the missionary in starting the church to depend on its own resources and to look unto itself for the solution of its own problems. Had the missionary opened her house and provided the chairs, the time would come when the missionary would leave and the Christians would have been unprepared to assume these simple responsibilities. Not only would they be unprepared, they would still be weak for whatever the missionary does encourages the Christians to remain babes as far as assuming responsibility is concerned.

Some American churches that seek to be easily accessible to the unchurched seeker wonder if they have made a mistake. Is this problem similar to the one in this passage, or different from it?

They would not have the privilege of doing things which would strengthen them in their own organic life. The Christians become resourceful and strong in the solution of these physical matters only as they are given the responsibility. The wise move and in fact, the New Testament procedure is to have the Christians undertake these things themselves from the very beginning. It has been found that the assuming of these responsibilities by the Christians at the very outset has strengthened them and increased their ability for self-propagation. Thus these simple factors contribute to the fulfilling of the three phases of indigenous work—self-supporting, self-governing, and self- propagating. As they provided a place of worship and its needs, they were self-supporting. This brought among them the use of a self-governing procedure. The very strength and interest encouraged by these activities made them more active in the self-propagating phase. In fact, because the Christians did these things, the surrounding villages saw and became more interested and attracted to the church services and thus were drawn to the Gospel message itself.

E. Well-established missions are turning more and more to indigenous principles

Recently a returned missionary spoke to a student body about the missionary policy of an outstanding mission. He mentioned that when a missionary went into a new territory and a new village he would find an empty building and rent it with his foreign funds. He would then go up and down the village area and preach the Gospel message. As soon as he gathered a group together, he would have them come to this rented building where they would study the Word of God. He would try to challenge them to become missionaries to their own people and would pay them money to come into the building at special hours to learn. This money also came from foreign funds.

Because of the funds they could pay, the missionaries would get quite a few people to come and study the Word of God. They did get some results in having the students go out and speak to their own people. At the conclusion of this survey of the work, the missionary said that this procedure had failed.

Recently they had to come face to face with the facts and on their faces before the Lord they had to tell the world that they, as a mission board, had failed the Chinese in not giving out the Gospel message as the Bible teaches them to do it. They have since revised their policy. From now on they will go as a group of six people into an area and will live in a building which will be completely filled and will not house anybody else. Therefore, no meetings can be held in this building in which the workers themselves would be living. They will go up and down the streets and preach the Gospel, but now they will not have a rented building. They will get the groups together, meeting at a place which the nationals themselves will provide. After the Christians have found the building they will be expected to pay the rent and take care of it by themselves. The missionaries will then teach the people. They feel that their method of giving missionary funds to the nationals in the past has been a complete failure. They have found this to be true because of the reports from their work since the Bamboo Curtain has dropped. It is reported that the only church from which they are now having reports concerning an active ministry is that which has been established among the Lisu people. The Lisu have used the "indigenous principles" as described in the book "Behind the Ranges." Beginning under Mr. Fraser they held strictly to indigenous principles. Although they were criticized by others, all now know this is the way missionary work should be carried on.

Another factor mentioned was that the missionary should not plan to stay permanently in one place, but should be continually moving. After a period of time, each group of six missionaries will move to another village or town, hoping in this way to carry out the plan as laid down in the Book of Acts. They believe now that the New Testament method of carrying out the Gospel message, the so-called "indigenous method," is one that is more effective and one that will continue to produce results after the missionary has left.

V. Steps in Developing an Indigenous Field

How can a missionary make his work indigenous? In general, the following steps give a logical pattern:

1. The foreign missionary comes with the Gospel. He plants the Gospel in the hearts and lives of men and women.

2. This Gospel, if it grows and bears fruit, will normally induce Christians anywhere to gather together in what is known as the New Testament church with a simple organization. The material needs of the church will be met by the members. The government and organization of the church will be by the national membership. The spread of the church after the first initial efforts of the missionary will be almost wholly the result of the local church members. If the Gospel has done its work in the life and heart of an individual, that one will be pressing forward to witness to and to evangelize those who do not have Christ in the immediate locality. This will be the source of growth for the local church.

3. When this stage has been reached, the missionary changes from being primarily an evangelist to becoming a teacher who instructs the babes in Christ.

4. In due process of time, any local group will, through the New Testament teachings, absorb the knowledge which will enable that church to be not only a soul-winning church, but also an instructor of Christians in the walk of a Christian life.

5. When this stage (No. 4) has been reached in the spiritual life of a church, the missionary will move on to plant a church in another area.

6. Another stage will be reached when there will be enough local churches to care for this pushing-out process. They will be sending their own folk out into the un-evangelized areas to establish the new churches. At this period, the missionary's main function will be that of a Bible teacher in some Bible training institution.

7. When the local constituency has been trained sufficiently to take over the teaching function of the Bible training schools, then the work of the missionary in that field is finished.

8. Institutions will find their place in the church planting and growth as follows:

    a. The institutions may be hospitals, clinics, dispensaries, leprosy colonies, sanitariums, orphanages, hostels, old folks' homes, schools, etc.

b. The more any institution is an outgrowth of the local church, the sounder will be its foundation.

c. The less foreign funds and staff are used, the sooner will the institution stand without the aid of a foreign scaffold as an integral part of the church.

d. Wherever foreign staff and resources are used in establishing, promoting and continuing an institution, it should be the avowed purpose to work toward a goal of making the institution independent of all foreign support, financial organization and incentive.

VI. Conclusion

The field policies for the Conservative Baptist Foreign Mission Society have not been permanently crystallized. The pattern which we form this year may be modified in the years ahead; modified by experience and because of growth and development on our various fields.

Although there is not full agreement as to the extent indigenous methods should be applied in detail, the last few years have brought certain decisions which are helping us to crystallize our thinking in certain areas of this important aspect of missionary work. By a process of study and experimentation we are slowly coming to the place where we agree on certain procedures basic to the indigenous approach. This paper is presented in the hope that it will stimulate our thinking on the subject and make us aware of the great issues involved.

The development of the indigenous policy is not a process of thought control and intellectual exercise by the Board and its missionaries. It is a Holy Spirit–guided process for establishing the church, and though we believe there are certain basic procedures that should be the same for all of our missionaries, we recognize that modifications are necessary with so many different fields and different missionaries. What may work in one place may not be desirable in another. What may work for one person may not be best for another. The Holy Spirit is not limited to a legalistic approach. The Holy Spirit will guide surrendered and yielded lives to that procedure which is the will of God. We are not interested as much in the indigenous approach as we are in the Holy Spirit–guided policy. We are of the opinion, however, as we have studied missions—historically and the immediate needs as well as our New Testament plans—that the Holy Spirit points toward a method which may generally be classified as indigenous.

VII. Supplement

Since the inception of our Society, the Board has voted various field policies which have committed us to certain methods in carrying on the task of presenting the Gospel to the unsaved in other lands. Last May, in order to further consider the so-called "indigenous approach" to missionary work, the Foreign Department prepared a paper "A Study of Indigenous Policies and Procedures" which was presented and partially discussed by the Board.

During the months following the presentation of this paper there have been comments from missionaries, pastors, and laymen regarding the merits and demerits of the suggestions set forth in it. The purpose of this brief paper is to consider some of the questions that have been asked and then to ask some questions to which the Board may wish to give serious consideration.

Questions People Are Asking

1. Are not the propositions set forth in the paper "A Study of Indigenous Policies and Procedures" too radical and too extreme to be worked out in practical form?

Comment: Not if various factors are kept in mind.

a. Most mission boards "talk" indigenous methods but often do not "do" too much about it because neither the home constituency nor, oftentimes, the missionary is sufficiently "sold" on the indigenous approach to exercise the self-discipline required to make the approach effective.

Too many times in their desire to give generously to the cause of missions, churches do not analyze the specific work for which their money is being used. Missionaries who are not "sold" on the indigenous approach can plan on the sympathies and humanitarian desires of the home constituency to secure things which the Board would not approve and which hold back the process of the indigenous approach. As a Board and Administrative Staff, to which the churches have committed the task of establishing churches in other lands, ours is the work of analyzing and drawing up certain policies which, in our estimation, will produce the greatest and most permanent results.

This supplement lists Argentina as one of the negative examples for the mission society's policy. On the whole, how indigenous do you think the efforts of the Gerows and Olsons were in the accounts above? Where is a thoroughly indigenous approach difficult, and why?

b. It has been demonstrated (Korea, China, Congo and Argentina) that the old method (subsidization from America) has often failed whereas the more indigenous the approach, the more permanent (though often slower) the results.

c. The indigenous approach is more in keeping with the nationalism which today is so prominent in various countries of the world.

2. Is not the CBFMS inconsistent in its approach to the same problems on different fields?

Comment: It is true that a casual knowledge of work on our various fields would lead to the conclusion that we are inconsistent. Here are some of the facts contributing to this apparent inconsistency.

a. *Conditions on the field making the modified approach necessary.* In India we were forced to take over hostels already in existence. In Congo the establishing of an educational system was one of the conditions which had to be met in order to work there. In both India and Congo leprosy colonies were made our responsibility.

b. *Commitments made by the Board before it knew what is best in the way of mission policies.* In Portugal, France and in Brazil we set up a plan in the early days of the Society whereby money was given to subsidize the work of the churches. That is now being gradually cut down and eventually will be entirely eliminated.

c. *Young people with "specialized" training apply to our Board.* Are we, as some Boards have done, to check those who come to us trained in subjects other than theology? Thus far we have chosen to accept them feeling that God would lead us in showing how and where they could fit into the framework of establishing the Church of Christ without undue violence to the indigenous approach.

d. *Diversity of thinking on the part of our missionary personnel.* It is to be expected that there will be different opinions concerning the indigenous approach on the part of our missionary family. Even if we all were agreed as to the goal, there could be serious differences of opinion as to how the goal could best be reached. Just as a father uses different methods on different children in order to achieve the same result (strong character, emotional stability, and spiritual maturity) so a mission board must be willing at times to be flexible enough to "adjust" to these differences of opinion without losing sight of the goal we are trying to attain. To that end we should be constantly challenging our missionaries to read books and then study the missionaries' programs in order to see where improvements can be made. A parent uses different approaches to the same child at different age levels in order to achieve the same results. So the mission board or conference may vary its approach at different times on the same field.

3. Will not the adherence to this policy lead to serious personality conflicts?

Comment: It is true that two individuals whose thinking is in the "philosophy of missionary methods" can have serious clashes. This would be true no matter what the Board's basic policy is. This factor calls for great wisdom on the part of the Home Board and Administrative Staff. Surely the answer is not to stifle thinking on the part of the missionaries. Neither is the answer found in giving in to the wishes of the missionaries without any guidance from the Home Board.

a. There must be mutual respect for the thinking and opinions of others even when these views do not coincide exactly with our own.

b. There must be a thorough briefing of all our appointees as to what we mean by the indigenous approach to missionary work and suggestions should be made as to how it can be best carried out.

c. When the Conference and Home Board have agreed upon a certain method of procedure, there should be a serious effort on the part of each missionary to follow the approved action of the group.

d. From time to time the Foreign Department, though apparently condoning certain "inconsistencies" on the indigenous approach, should by question and suggestion, challenge all of the missionaries to strive for the goal of making their work completely indigenous or New Testament.

Source: Used by permission.

PART THREE
ASSISTING THE INVESTIGATION

Why Study Conservative Baptists in Northwest Argentina? Suggestions for Devotional Use

The following are suggestions for devotional use that correspond with specific sections of the book:

Describing the Community's Worship:
Argentine Baptists, Mid-Twentieth Century

- The primary work of CBFMS missionaries was to communicate the gospel message to the "ends of the earth." Investigate local and global missionaries you might know through your church or another mission agency. Locate them on a map of the world. Read about their work, pray for them, and consider ways you might partner in their ministry.
- Find a map of the world and hang it in a prominent place. Use this map to pray for missionaries in different countries on each continent by marking their location as you learn about and pray for their work.
- The Argentines the CBFMS missionaries encountered were often hearing the gospel for the first time. Remember the time you first heard the gospel story. What was the setting? Who told you that story? What gave you hope? What questions did you have?
- Put yourself in the shoes of an Argentine in the middle of the twentieth century. Imagine the challenges of living in a country wracked by economic instability, political unrest, and at times an uncertain future. What might have been happening in your mind, your body, your spirit, and your soul? Read through the words of "Peace, What a Peace!" written by the youth group in Tucumán (p. 103). What words would bring you hope as an Argentine in the middle of the twentieth century?
- The Great Commission (Matt. 28:16–20) served as an impetus for missionaries like the Gerows and Olsons. In this passage, after Jesus tells his disciples to "Go into all the world," Jesus promises that he will be with his disciples until the very end of the age. How does this promise bring you hope as you seek to be a disciple of Christ in your everyday work?

People and Artifacts

- Ronald Olson compiled a list of the baptisms he performed over a two-year period in the towns of Prediliana, Maiz Negro, and Libertador—often in irrigation ditches through full immersion. Recall your baptism. Where was it? Who was there? Read the story of Jesus's baptism in Matthew 3:13–17, and spend time reminding yourself of your baptism's significance today.
- In the photographs, both the Baptist missionaries and the Argentines often reflect a spirit of joy in their worship, prayer, and praise. Browse the Psalms and find three joyful statements (e.g., "You show me the way of life, granting me joy"). Write down two or three of these passages to help you recall them when you need to be reminded of the joy that comes from the Lord.

Worship Setting and Space

- Worship among the Argentine Baptists happened in many places other than church buildings: homes, tents, roadsides, and irrigation ditches. Recall a time when you worshiped in an "uncommon" space. Where was it? What sights and sounds do you recall? How did this worship, outside the walls of the church, shape your understanding of worship inside the church?
- Worship in Argentine homes might have been uncomfortable, especially when more than sixty people crowded into one person's home. Make a list of the things that make you "comfortable" in worship (pew, personal space, music, etc.). Have you sacrificed, or would you sacrifice, personal comfort to be with other Christians? What on your list would you be willing to give up? What would be difficult for you to give up?

Descriptions of Worship

- The Easter Conference was one of the most significant worship events described in the firsthand accounts. It often lasted three or more days, with more than twenty meetings, and its primary purpose was "soul winning." Read a journal entry about one of the Easter Conferences; then write a description of your own worship practices before, during, and after Easter. What makes them different from worship at other times of the year? What makes them special to you?

Worship Texts

- Read through the late nineteenth- and early twentieth-century hymns the Argentine Baptists used. Choose a text that is meaningful to you, and read about the history of this hymn on a Web site such as http://www.hymnary.org/.
- Memorize one of the worship choruses written by an Argentine, learning it as poetry only.

Sermons

- Read the outline of Ronald Olson's sermon on the Lord's Supper, and look up the key passages referenced. Note the number of times the word "body" appears in the sermon outline and in the Scripture passages. What different meanings is this word assigned in Olson's sermon and in Scripture? How does this inform your personal understanding of the body of Christ?
- Ronald Olson's Christmas sermon on Isaiah 9 asks a series of questions such as "Is Jesus Christ wonderful to you?" and "Is Jesus Christ your Counselor . . . Mighty God . . . Everlasting Father . . . Prince of Peace?" and concludes with the question, "Is Christ all this for us?" Spend time reflecting on these questions, and make a list of the ways you, or those you know, have experienced Christ in these capacities.

Theology of Worship Documents

- The Bible was an important source of wisdom and authority regarding the church and its worship practices for the CBFMS missionaries. What, besides Scripture, informs your understanding of the church and its worship practices?

Why Study Conservative Baptists in Northwest Argentina? Discussion Questions for Small Groups

The following are discussion questions for each section of this book.

General Introduction and Timeline

- What did you learn about Christianity in Argentina in the middle of the twentieth century?
- What is your experience with foreign missions in the church? Have foreign missions changed since the middle of the twentieth century? Why or why not?
- How might foreign mission practices strengthen the local and global church? Are there ways that foreign mission practices might have hurt the local and global church?
- It is often believed, or assumed, that Catholics and Protestants have competing practices. What did you observe about the relationship between Catholics and Protestants in Argentina? How does that compare to your understanding of Catholics and Protestants today?

Describing the Community's Worship

- What would it have been like to worship in a northwest Argentina church in the mid-twentieth century? How have you seen cultural, political, and socioeconomic issues impact worship in the church?
- What challenges do you think the missionaries faced when interacting and worshiping with people who spoke a different native language, had different cultural backgrounds, and had different religious traditions? What opportunities for cultural sharing might both sides have experienced?
- What is the relationship between evangelism and worship? Why do you think the Baptist missionaries used the number of converts to determine whether worship was successful? How does your congregation determine whether or not your worship practices are efficacious?

- Do you think testifying, a worship element common among Baptists and Pentecostals, has a place in worship practices today? Why or why not?
- How did the Baptist missionaries' understanding of congregational autonomy help their work in establishing congregations in Argentina?

People and Artifacts

- What challenges did the Gerows and Olsons face when they began their work in Argentina? Could they have alleviated those challenges by doing something prior to arriving in Argentina? Why or why not?
- On occasion, the missionary journals describe challenges such as religious indifference or a "dry period." Have you or your church ever experienced a "dry period"? What did that period feel like? Was it overcome? If so, how?
- What would it be like to worship with individuals of a very different social class than yours? What cultural, theological, and other challenges might such an instance present?
- "Jesus Christ as the Savior sent by God to find sinners" was the recurring theme of the Baptist missionaries' work and worship. Is there a recurring theme in the worship practices in which you participate? If so, what is it, and how prominent is it?
- Do you think the tools the CBFMS missionaries used such as music, preaching, puppets, testimony, and tracts were effective? Why or why not? What tools or practices does your congregation use to communicate the gospel? Music? Preaching? Testimony? Baptism? Communion? How are these used?

Worship Setting and Space

- What would it have been like to worship "crowded like sardines" in a home? What would it have been like to worship outside in a tent? What would it have been like to celebrate the Easter Conference as a group of Protestants when a Catholic procession for Good Friday passed on the street?
- Why is the construction of a church building important for a worshiping community? What value might come from the worshipers constructing such a building themselves, as opposed to hiring laborers to construct the building?

Descriptions of Worship

- How often does your worshiping community celebrate the Lord's Supper? What might be gained or lost by celebrating it more or less frequently?
- Most Baptists do not observe the Lord's Supper weekly, yet the Baptist missionaries did not change this practice carried over from the Plymouth Brethren. What does this say about the Argentine Baptists' understanding of tradition? How is tradition helpful to a worshiping community? How can tradition hinder a worshiping community?
- The American practice of a "sunrise service" on Easter Sunday did not work well in Argentina. What are possible reasons? Did other American worship practices not work with the Christians in Argentina? How did the missionaries adapt their American practices to work better among Argentine Christians?

Worship Texts

- Would it have been difficult for Argentines to learn and sing nineteenth- and twentieth-century hymns such as "The Ninety and Nine" the Baptists used in worship? Why or why not?
- Many of the nineteenth- and twentieth-century hymns the congregation sang focused on evangelism, mission, and witness. What is the value of focusing on these themes in worship? Is it possible to focus too much on evangelism and witness in worship? How do you find an appropriate balance?
- What did you learn about Argentine Christianity from the texts of the indigenous worship choruses? In today's culture, where worship music is saturated by marketing to consumers, is there value in local congregations writing and singing their own music in worship?
- Are extemporaneous testimonies, prayers, and in some cases worship orders any more genuine than testimonies, prayers, and worship orders that are written down? Why or why not?

Sermons

- How might it have been different to hear Ronald Olson and others preach, compared to reading outlines of sermons?
- Do you notice any prominent themes in Olson's sermon outlines? What are they?

Theology of Worship Documents

- What distinct features of the church does Ronald Olson uphold in his Bible study outline given to Ledesma Baptists? How might Olson's ecclesiology, and that of the other CBFMS missionaries, have differed from the ecclesiology of the Catholics and native Argentines at the time?
- After reading about worship among Argentine Baptists and reading Olson's lessons on the nature of the church, where do you see congruence between these Baptists' worship practices and beliefs? How do your beliefs about the church inform your beliefs about worship, and vice versa?

Polity Documents

- The polity documents from CBFMS suggest an openness to worship that reflects the local culture. How does your church's worship reflect your local culture? Are there pieces of that culture that are omitted? How might you include them?
- It is clear that personal evangelism is an important distinctive for CBFMS missionaries. What are important distinctives within your denomination? Among its missionaries?

Why Study Conservative Baptists in Northwest Argentina? A Guide for Different Disciplines and Areas of Interest

Christianity

If you are interested in Christianity as a religion generally, then Conservative Baptists in northwest Argentina are helpful for understanding the following:

- missionary movement, methods, and impulse in the twentieth century;
- relationship between Catholics and Protestants in Argentina;
- the growth and rise of Christianity in the Global South; and
- connections between culture and religion.

Here are discussion questions based on these general religious issues:

- What propelled Christians to become "career missionaries," seeking and saving the lost?
- In the broader landscape of twentieth-century missionary movements, what niche did CBFMS missionaries like the Gerows and Olsons fill?
- What enabled Argentines from different social classes (e.g., those from the middle class and those in poverty) to worship side by side?
- How did the Baptist missionaries overcome oppression from the government, Argentine Catholics, and nonbelievers to propel their mission forward?

Christian Worship

If you are interested in worship generally, then Conservative Baptists in northwest Argentina are helpful for understanding the following:

- worship that is transcultural, contextual, countercultural, and cross-cultural, and all the inherent promises and challenges associated with each;
- liturgical inculturation, acculturation, and contextualization;
- worship as a means of evangelism and baptizing new Christians; and
- the centrality of preaching, singing, testifying, and evangelizing in Baptist worship practices.

Here are discussion questions based on these general worship issues:

- Read the "Nairobi Statement on Worship and Culture," which defines transcultural, contextual, countercultural, and cross-cultural worship (http://worship.calvin.edu /resources/resource-library/nairobi-statement-on-worship-and-culture-full-text). At what points was the worship by Conservative Baptists in northwest Argentina transcultural? Contextual? Countercultural? Cross-cultural?
- Has a greater awareness of liturgical inculturation better informed cross-cultural worship practices, particularly where missionaries are concerned?
- How do worship practices that are so centered on one's personal relationship with Christ accomplish the act of telling the cosmic story of the gospel while also offering thanks and praise to the triune God?

Music

If you are interested in music, then Conservative Baptists in northwest Argentina are helpful for understanding the following:

- the use of music in foreign missions as a method of evangelism;
- the centrality of Jesus Christ in evangelical hymnody;
- dominant themes in nineteenth- and twentieth-century gospel hymnody; and
- the value of indigenous music in missions and its possible implications for the field of ethnomusicology.

Here are discussion questions based on these music issues:

- Why have the worship choruses composed and used by the Argentine Baptists not become "popular" and widely used by other Christians, as occurs with many other worship choruses?

- How might an understanding of ethnomusicology, and even the presence of an ethno-musicologist, have enhanced the liturgical musical life of Argentine Baptists?
- Why were nineteenth- and twentieth-century hymns so prominent among missionaries, not only to Argentina, but also to other countries?
- Which themes do you think are most prominent in the hymns sung by Argentine Baptists? (Jesus Christ? Lost souls? Christians? Heaven?)

Spirituality

If you are interested in spirituality, then Conservative Baptists in northwest Argentina are helpful for understanding the following:

- Scripture as the supreme source of authority among Baptists and evangelicals;
- the importance of a personal relationship with Jesus Christ;
- the role of an individual conversion experience followed by believer's baptism; and
- the emphasis upon a visible, local church.

Here are discussion questions based on these spirituality issues:

- How did these Baptists use Scripture as a source of authority in their personal devotion, worship practices, and mission endeavors?
- While the Argentine Baptists worshiped in homes, tents, and streets and performed baptisms in irrigation ditches, why was the construction of a visible church building so important to them?

Church History

If you are interested in church history, then Conservative Baptists in northwest Argentina are helpful for understanding the following:

- the history of Northern Baptists in the United States;
- the rise and importance of missions among Baptists in the United States, as well as other denominations, in the twentieth century;
- the development of the Conservative Baptist Foreign Mission Society and other similar groups coming out of denominational factions; and

- controversies between conservatives and liberals in the United States throughout the twentieth century.

Here are discussion questions based on these church history issues:

- How did divisions between and within denominations affect their missionary activities? How did they affect their worship practices?
- How has the work of CBFMS missionaries such as the Gerows and Olsons continued in Argentina and beyond? What factors contributed to their success of spreading the gospel in this part of the world?
- If these Baptist missionaries were still serving today, what practices do you think they would keep? What might they change?

Glossary of Bolded Terms

Asado Argentine version of a barbecue.

Cena Spanish word for supper, used in this book to refer to the Lord's Supper or communion.

Colporteur Someone who distributes printed religious material.

Conquistador A leader in the Spanish conquests, especially of Mexico and Peru in the sixteenth century.

Corpus Christi Latin for the body of Christ. It refers to the feast in the Roman Catholic calendar that celebrates the consecrated communion as the body of Christ. It occurs on the Thursday after Trinity Sunday, the first Sunday after the feast of Pentecost (fifty days after Easter).

Easter Conference Regional worship, evangelism, and education meeting that Baptists in northwest Argentina would hold annually from the Thursday before Easter to Easter Sunday.

Evangelical As used in this book, a broad term that refers to a kind of conservative, Protestant Christianity characterized by evangelism, personal experiences of conversion, and an emphasis on the Bible as the key authority for individuals and churches. It is a broader term than "free church" or "fundamentalist," although it encompasses both.

Flannel graph Presentational tool that uses a felt backdrop and felt cutouts of characters/objects. It is often used to tell Bible stories. The felt adheres to itself, and so the characters and objects can be easily moved around the backdrop.

Free church Although the term can be used generally to refer to a church that refuses to conform to the norms of an established church, in this book it refers to those churches that practice freedom to reform worship on the basis of Scripture without reference to tradition. This freedom is usually exercised by each worshiping community locally as it orders worship.

Fundamentalist Someone who upholds a strict and literal interpretation of Scripture. This term as an adjective describes such an approach to the Bible.

Good Friday Annual feast in the liturgical calendar that commemorates the crucifixion of Christ. It comes two days before Easter. Among some Roman Catholics, it is an occasion for public liturgical processions.

Gospel hymn A hymn that originated in nineteenth-century congregational song. Such hymns were often known as "white gospel music" or "white spirituals," and their origin can be traced to mass evangelism approaches during the Second Great Awakening.

Immaculate Conception of the Virgin Mary Annual feast that remembers the conception of Mary, the mother of Jesus, on December 8. Her conception is considered immaculate in the sense that she was free from original sin when conceived, according to Roman Catholic doctrine.

Ingenio Spanish word for a factory or sugar refinery.

Liturgical inculturation Process and dynamics by which Christian worship is influenced by its surrounding culture.

Lote A small, company-owned village associated with sugarcane plantations.

Lotero Spanish word for a boss; in this book it refers to the management of sugar refineries.

Mate Pronounced ma-tay, this is a highly popular drink in South America. It is made by steeping dry leaves of yerba mate in hot water, producing a stimulating drink (scientific opinions differ as to whether it contains caffeine or mateine) that is an important part of social gatherings.

Mestizos People of mixed European and indigenous non-European ancestry.

Missiology The study of the principles and practices of religious missions, particularly those within Christianity.

Pentecostalism A form of evangelical Protestantism that emphasizes a variety of ecstatic phenomena, including baptism of the Holy Spirit, speaking in tongues, healing, and miracles. The term also applies to a person who abides by this form of Christianity.

Plymouth Brethren A small, conservative, British-originated movement that carried out some of the earliest missionary work in northwest Argentina. It is largely evangelical in character. In Argentina adherents were known as *Hermanos Libres*, that is, Free Brethren. Seeking to follow biblical guidelines on how to conduct worship meetings, the movement has weekly communion, no classes of lay or clergy, and a restriction against women speaking in worship, among other elements.

Sunday school Religious classes held by a church on Sunday morning.

Testimony (or testifying) Speaking about how one has experienced the grace of God, especially the saving work of Jesus Christ, and has been changed by the experience.

Bibliography and Suggestions
for Further Study

To Learn More about Christian Worship in the Twentieth Century

Berger, Teresa, and Bryan D. Spinks, eds. *The Spirit in Worship—Worship in the Spirit*. Collegeville, MN: Liturgical Press, 2009.

This collection of essays includes voices from theology, history, and practice who
work together to retrieve the doctrine of the Holy Spirit in the field of liturgical studies.
The cumulative effect of this collection is a vibrant and diverse articulation of the Holy
Spirit in worship and in faith. It will be helpful to those readers interested in exploring
the Pentecostal and charismatic influences that were prevalent in Argentina in the twentieth century.

Ellis, Christopher J. *Gathering: A Theology and Spirituality of Worship in Free Church Tradition*.
London: SCM, 2004.

Christopher Ellis's work is not unlike this volume in the Church at Worship series.
Ellis focuses on the narrative of Baptists in Great Britain. Ellis draws general conclusions
about Baptist worship from the work of liturgical scholar Alexander Schmemann. Ellis's
text is the most thorough of a handful of texts on Baptist worship practices, and readers
of this text will find his broad categories of devotion, Scripture, community, and kingdom
a useful lens for interpreting the liturgical values of the Argentine Baptists.

Fenwick, John R. K., and Bryan D. Spinks. *Worship in Transition: The Liturgical Movement in
the Twentieth Century*. New York: Continuum, 1995.

This text provides a helpful overview of the many liturgical changes that occurred
during the twentieth century, including, but not limited to, Vatican II. Readers interested
in the liturgical context of the CBFMS missionaries will find this text helpful for thinking
about the relationship between Protestant and Catholic worshiping communities. If read
with the above timeline (pp. 6–9) nearby, this text might provide an interesting comparison of the local and global contexts of worshipers in Argentina and around the world.

Flannery, Austin, OP, ed. *Vatican Council II: The Conciliar and Post Conciliar Documents*. New rev. ed. Collegeville, MN: Liturgical Press, 1996.

> This compilation, edited by a Dominican priest, is a massive but useful resource for understanding the specific impact Vatican II had on the Catholic Church worldwide. The documents themselves are accessible, and the sections on ecumenism, missionaries, worship, and music are necessary primary sources for anyone studying the work of the Catholic Church from 1962 onward.

Senn, Frank C. *Christian Liturgy: Catholic and Evangelical*. Minneapolis: Fortress, 1997.

> This book is an overview of Catholic and evangelical worship practices. Catholic practices are deeply rooted in the Christian tradition, while evangelical practices are centered on the gospel. Senn, a Lutheran minister, utilizes comparative liturgies to bring together historical, biblical, theological, anthropological, and musicological components of worship. Covering the entire scope of Christian worship history, this text will be a reference for understanding various points in worship history that might have influenced worship in Argentina.

Wainwright, Geoffrey, and Karen B. Westerfield Tucker, eds. *The Oxford History of Christian Worship*. New York: Oxford University Press, 2006.

> Edited by theologian Wainwright and historian Tucker, this large volume by multiple authors provides snapshots of worship throughout the centuries. Two articles, "Roman Catholics in Hispanic America" and "Mainline Protestants in Latin America," will be of particular interest to readers hoping to explore the historical and sociological challenges and opportunities these diverse groups found in the Global South.

To Better Understand Christianity in South America and Argentina

Canclini, Arnoldo. *400 Años de Protestantismo Argentino*. Buenos Aires: Facultad Internacional de Educación Teológica, 2004.

> Arnoldo Canclini was a Latin American pastor and noted church historian and theologian. He served the Baptist and evangelical communities inside and outside of Argentina. *400 Años de Protestantismo Argentino* is a lengthy history that documents the growing presence of evangelical missionaries in Argentina during the twentieth century.

Childs, Harwood L. "The Constitutions of the Latin American Republics." In *Consultation on Religious Liberty in Latin America*, part 2. New York: National Council of the Churches of Christ in the USA, 1955.

Childs provides a short, mid-twentieth-century review of the state of religiosity and opportunity for religions in various countries in Latin America. His work includes a summary of data compiled from a field survey conducted by the Committee on Cooperation in Latin America of the Division of Foreign Missions of the National Council of the Churches of Christ in the United States of America.

Enns, Arno W. *Man, Milieu, and Mission in Argentina: A Close Look at Church Growth*. Grand Rapids: Eerdmans, 1971.

Written by a conservative Baptist missionary to Argentina in the mid-twentieth century, this work documents ten Protestant churches in Argentina and their relationship to the Catholic Church, and assesses the factors that contributed to the rise of the evangelical community in Argentina. Part scholarship, part testimony, part admonition, Enns's text is one of the most comprehensive works on missions in the region in the twentieth century.

Gerow, C. D., and Janet Gerow. *Letters from Huacalera*. Privately published, 1996.

This is a privately published anthology of documents written by the Gerows. It includes letters asking for support and prayers from supporters in the United States. The letters kept these supporters informed about the state of the ministry and the life of the Gerow family.

Olson, Ronald, comp. *Cantemos*. Salta, Argentina: Privately published, n.d.

This is a collection of songs composed by Argentine Baptists in the twentieth century, compiled by Ronald Olson and used in his church. Examples of the song texts are cited earlier in this volume.

Rock, David. *Argentina, 1516–1982: From Spanish Colonization to the Falklands War*. Berkeley: University of California Press, 1985.

David Rock is a Latin American historian who specializes in Argentina. This comprehensive work covers the early colonial history of Argentina, explores the faltering of Argentina's ties with Europe following World War II, and traces the country's economic and political crisis in the later twentieth century.

For Background on the Conservative Baptist Foreign Mission Society

American Baptist Churches USA: http://www.abc-usa.org/.

    The American Baptist Churches USA (formerly the Northern Baptist Convention) is the denomination from which the Conservative Baptist Foreign Mission Society was born. While these two groups are no longer connected, it is interesting to compare the evolution of mission practices within the American Baptist Churches to those of CBAmerica and WorldVenture (listed below), the modern-day version of CBFMS.

CBAmerica: A Church-Based Network of Missional Ministries: http://cbamerica.org/.

    This is the Web site of the network of Conservative Baptists; it contains more information on the polity and network of Baptist churches that supported missionaries such as the Gerows and Olsons in their work. A visit to a church connected with CBAmerica will allow you to see the ongoing work of this denomination. You can find a list of congregations at http://cbamerica.org/connect/church-search/. As you examine the work of this agency, note that it, along with its foreign mission practices, has evolved from the time the Gerows and Olsons were on the field.

[Conservative Baptist Foreign Mission Society.] *Founded on the Word, Focused on the World: The Story of the Conservative Baptist Foreign Mission Society*. Wheaton, IL: Conservative Baptist Foreign Mission Society, 1978.

    This narrative tells how the CBFMS came to be and examines its work in the twentieth century until 1978.

Finzel, Hans W., ed. *Partners Together: 50 Years of Global Impact; The CBFMS Story, 1943–1993*. Wheaton, IL: Conservative Baptist Foreign Mission Society, 1993.

    Partners Together examines the work of CBFMS from 1943 to 1993, and was published to commemorate the fiftieth anniversary of CBFMS. This history traces the development of CBFMS from its inception until its transition to CBInternational in the final decade of the twentieth century.

Shelley, Bruce L. *A History of Conservative Baptists*. Wheaton, IL: Conservative Baptist Press, 1971.

    Dr. Bruce Shelley, longtime professor of church history and historical theology at Denver Seminary, has documented the history of Conservative Baptists in the United States. Specifically, Shelley traces the development of the Conservative Baptist Association of America. This text will be a useful companion for learning about the work of CBFMS as well as other parallel organizations and denominations that arose from theological conflict within the Northern Baptist Convention during the middle of the twentieth century.

WorldVenture: A Global Catalyst for Gospel Movements: https://www.worldventure.com/.

 WorldVenture was formerly known as the Conservative Baptist Foreign Mission Society (1943), and later as CBInternational (1994). It became WorldVenture in the early twenty-first century and relocated its office to Littleton, Colorado. This Web site provides more information on this agency and its approach to missions in the twenty-first century. Consider how this organization has adapted its missionary practices in the last fifty or sixty years.

To See Different Views on Foreign Missions History, Theology, and Practice

Akinade, Akintunde E., ed. *A New Day: Essays on World Christianity in Honor of Lamin Sanneh.* New York: Peter Lang, 2010.

 A New Day is a collection of essays in honor of Lamin Sanneh, who is described as "one of the most adamant advocates and apostles of radical change in the face of Christianity in the twenty-first century." These essays cover major themes, issues, and perspectives that are helpful for understanding Christianity as a global religious movement in which neither the West nor the North can be seen as the primary harbinger of the Christian faith.

Barnes, Jonathan S. "The Ambivalence of Partnership: A Colonial and Contested History." *Encounter* 74, no. 3 (Summer 2014): 27–44.

 Mission work is often described as a partnership. In this essay, former missionary to South Africa and Mozambique Jonathan Barnes traces the development of this word in light of the history of Protestant mission. Barnes suggests that the term has been both ambivalent and contested because it is rooted in colonialism, a concept that has little meaning in the twenty-first century, where missions are international and ecumenical.

Bosch, David J. *Transforming Mission: Paradigm Shifts in Theology of Mission.* Maryknoll, NY: Orbis, 1991.

 Transforming Mission is a voluminous historical, theological, and practical resource covering the span of missions from biblical accounts to the present day. Bosch traces five dominant paradigms of mission movements, then provides a framework for understanding missions in a postmodern epoch. Readers of this text will better understand the shifts in foreign missions that took place before, during, and after the work of the Gerows and Olsons in Argentina.

Dilley, Andrea Palpant. "The World the Missionaries Made." *Christianity Today* 51, no. 1 (January/February 2014): 34–41.

  In this journal article, Dilley provides an overview of sociologist Robert Woodberry's work (see below), which shows how the modern mission movement had a strong, positive influence on liberal democratization. This resource is a helpful introduction to this important sociologist's work.

Sanneh, Lamin. *Translating the Message: The Missionary Impact on Culture*. Maryknoll, NY: Orbis, 1989.

  In this seminal work on missiology, Sanneh emphasizes the importance of reception and adaptation of the gospel message on the mission field, as opposed to the translation of the gospel. Sanneh uses Pentecost as a historical frame of reference before tracing the development and proliferation of missions to communicate a gospel of grace.

Walls, Andrew F. *The Missionary Movement in Christian History: Studies in the Transmission of Faith*. Maryknoll, NY: Orbis, 1996.

  The collected lectures, articles, and thoughts of Andrew Walls, noted missionary and historian, can be read as a sympathetic counterpart to Sanneh's work (see above), in that both appreciate the diverse forms of Christianity and culture that arise, sometimes unintentionally, in missionary work.

Westhelle, Vítor. *After Heresy: Colonial Practices and Postcolonial Theologies*. Eugene, OR: Cascade Books, 2010.

  As an important overview of colonial missionary practices in Latin America, the "crisis" of Western modernity, and postcolonial mission practices applicable to the twenty-first century, this text is helpful for understanding the shifting dynamics and practices of CBFMS, CBInternational, and now WorldVenture.

Woodberry, Robert D. "The Missionary Roots of Liberal Democracy." *American Political Science Review* 106, no. 2 (May 2012): 244–74.

  Sociologist Robert Woodberry makes a strong case, historically and statistically, that Protestant missionaries made a significant contribution to a stable democracy in the regions where their work was prevalent. The cumulative effect of their work has been a catalyst in initiating religious liberty, mass education, literacy, and other colonial reforms.

To Be Aware of the Breadth of Global Christianity in the Twentieth Century

González, Justo L. *The Story of Christianity*. Vol. 1, *The Early Church to the Dawn of the Reformation*. 2nd ed. San Francisco: HarperOne, 2010.

>   Justo González is both a theologian and a historian. *The Story of Christianity* is a narrative history of Christianity from the early church to the present day. The fourth part of this first volume will be helpful for understanding the beginning of colonial Christianity in Argentina, Brazil, and beyond.

González, Justo L. *The Story of Christianity*. Vol. 2, *The Reformation to the Present Day*. 2nd ed. San Francisco: HarperOne, 2010.

>   This volume continues González's historical narrative from the Reformation to the present day. Part 2 provides the context for growing Protestantism and Catholicism in the United States, while part 3 is helpful for understanding the current "shifting landscape" of Christianity in the world, mentioned often by the Baptist missionaries in northwest Argentina.

Jenkins, Philip. *The New Faces of Christianity: Believing the Bible in the Global South*. New York: Oxford University Press, 2008.

>   In this work Jenkins traces the transmission, acceptance, and adaptation of the Bible in areas of the Global South such as Argentina. Many in that region, Jenkins claims, were taught literal interpretations of Scripture but have adapted those teachings to speak to their present and often challenging third world circumstances. The result has been an amalgamation of biblical principles that transcends dichotomies found in the Global North.

Jenkins, Philip. *The Next Christendom: The Coming of Global Christianity*. 3rd ed. New York: Oxford University Press, 2011.

>   In this text Jenkins documents the shifting landscape of Christianity from the Global North to the Global South. An accessible text, *The Next Christendom* is a must-read for those hoping to understand this shift as well as those hoping to do cross-cultural ministry in the twenty-first century.

Noll, Mark. *Turning Points: Decisive Moments in the History of Christianity*. 3rd ed. Grand Rapids: Baker Academic, 2012.

>   *Turning Points* by Mark Noll, noted historian of American evangelicalism and Christianity, provides snapshots in Christian history that transformed Christianity on a macro

level. The final two chapters will help readers of *Leaning on the Word* understand the impact of the Protestant missionary movement and Vatican II on the twentieth century.

For Background on the History and Theology of Baptists in the United States

Bush, L. Russ, and Tom J. Nettles. *Baptists and the Bible*. Rev. ed. Nashville: Broadman and Holman, 1999.

> *Baptists and the Bible* provides a narrative of beliefs that Baptists in England and the United States have held about the Bible. It is a wonderfully useful resource for researchers and scholars interested in learning more about the "bibliology" of Baptists in the Northern Baptist Convention, now the American Baptist Churches USA, and formerly the sending arm of the CBFMS.

Hatch, Nathan O. *The Democratization of American Christianity*. New Haven: Yale University Press, 1989.

> CBFMS missionaries to Argentina were undoubtedly influenced in zeal and effort by the breed of American Christianity that followed the Second Great Awakening. *The Democratization of American Christianity* traces the spirit and ethos of nineteenth-century religious movements in the United States, especially those tied to missions inside the United States, including a large number of Baptists in the North and South. Readers of *Leaning on the Word* may find some similarities between the spirit of missions in Argentina and the earliest centuries of the United States.

Marsden, George M. *Understanding Fundamentalism and Evangelicalism*. Grand Rapids: Eerdmans, 1991.

> Fundamentalism and evangelicalism are ideas that figured prominently in twentieth-century Christianity, especially in the work of the CBFMS. Here George Marsden, an expert on each, provides a historical overview of these two themes, including their primary tenets and their development and rise in Christianity.

McBeth, H. Leon. *The Baptist Heritage: Four Centuries of Baptist Witness*. Nashville: Broadman Press, 1987.

> *The Baptist Heritage* is a dense resource that outlines more than four hundred years of Baptist history. Beginning with precursors to Baptists' separation from the Church of England in the seventeenth century, well-known historian Leon McBeth traces the work of this influential denomination both chronologically and topically.

Norman, R. Stanton. *The Baptist Way: Distinctives of a Baptist Church*. Nashville: Broadman and Holman, 2005.

>   Historically, Baptist individuals and congregations have identified themselves by a number of distinctives, such as biblical authority, the Lordship of Jesus Christ, a regenerate church membership, church discipline, congregational autonomy, baptism and the Lord's Supper as ordinances, and religious freedom. In this primer, Norman provides an overview of these distinctives, many of which can be traced through the work of the CBFMS missionaries and their congregations in Argentina.

To Explore the Relationships between Worship and Culture

Black, Kathy. *Culturally-Conscious Worship*. St. Louis: Chalice, 2000.

>   *Culturally-Conscious Worship* is philosophical, theological, sociological, but most of all pastoral. It provides helpful definitions, models, values, and complexities that arise when people of different cultures worship together. A number of stories and case studies illustrate the principles woven throughout this book with immense pastoral care.

Black, Kathy. *Worship Across Cultures: A Handbook*. Nashville: Abingdon, 1998.

>   This text is a companion to *Culturally-Conscious Worship*. Readers of *Leaning on the Word* will find sections on Hispanic American worship and Latin American worship useful for better understanding the ministry of the Gerows and Olsons in Argentina.

Chupungco, Anscar J. *Liturgical Inculturation: Sacramentals, Religiosity, and Catechesis*. Collegeville, MN: Liturgical Press, 1992.

>   Chupungco is an influential Roman Catholic liturgical scholar who has studied worship and culture. His work has been influential among Protestants and is particularly helpful for understanding the liturgical narrative of Baptist missionaries in Argentina.

Farhadian, Charles E., ed. *Christian Worship Worldwide: Expanding Horizons, Deepening Practices*. Grand Rapids: Eerdmans, 2007.

>   Drawing upon a strong range of authors who reflect both different academic disciplines and familiarity with various parts of the world, this volume explores the interaction between culture and worship. The authors provide both analysis and case studies as they investigate how worship becomes a showcase for Christian plurality and difference.

González, Justo L., ed. *¡Alabadle! Hispanic Christian Worship*. Nashville: Abingdon, 1996.

>   González, mentioned above for his historical narrative of Christianity, is an impor-

tant historian and theologian. A Cuban American Methodist, he has written extensively on Christian history, Latino theology, as well as worship in the Hispanic tradition. This interdisciplinary text brings together his work, as well as the work of other experts, to provide an overview of worship in the Hispanic tradition.

Hawn, C. Michael. *Gather into One: Praying and Singing Globally*. Grand Rapids: Eerdmans, 2003.

> Michael Hawn is known all over the world for his work as a scholar, liturgist, and musician. *Gather into One* provides an extensive look at global worship practices that revolve around singing and praying for the sake of the world. Of particular interest to *Leaning on the Word* readers is chapter 2, a narrative of a theologian and song leader from Argentina, Pablo Sosa.

Hawn, C. Michael, ed. *New Songs of Celebration Render: Congregational Song in the Twenty-First Century*. Chicago: GIA Publications, 2013.

> *New Songs of Celebration Render* is a thorough overview of congregational song in the twenty-first century. The seventh chapter of this work provides a regional focus on hymnody in South America. How has the congregational song of this region changed since the Gerows and Olsons were there?

Hawn, C. Michael. *One Bread, One Body: Exploring Cultural Diversity in Worship*. Lanham, MD: Rowman and Littlefield, 2003.

> Similar to Kathy Black's work above, *One Bread, One Body* is a primer on cross-cultural worship. When people of different cultures come together in worship, should it be a melting pot or a mosaic? This book answers that question and gives biblical, theological, and pastoral attention to honoring all cultures in worship whether they are present or not.

Krabill, James R., ed. *Worship and Mission for the Global Church: An Ethnodoxology Handbook*. Pasadena, CA: William Carey Library, 2013.

> *Worship and Mission for the Global Church* is meant to be a handbook for ethnodoxologists, people who study the worship of cultures. This book features dozens of voices from a variety of perspectives discussing music, Scripture, liturgy, mission, and the arts in congregations around the world.

Lutheran World Federation. "The Lutheran World Federation's Nairobi Statement on Worship and Culture." In *New Directions in Mission and Evangelization 3: Faith and Culture*, edited by James A. Scherer and Stephen B. Bevans, 177–84. Maryknoll, NY: Orbis, 1999.

> The "Nairobi Statement on Worship and Culture" is a historical document that

should be a touchstone for every student, minister, and scholar examining the relationship between worship and culture. Written by the Lutheran World Federation in January of 1996 in Nairobi, this document presents four principles for navigating worship that is transcultural, contextual, countercultural, and cross-cultural.

Witvliet, John D. "Theological and Conceptual Models for Liturgy and Culture." *Liturgy Digest* 3, no. 2 (1996): 5–46.

This article by John Witvliet examines approaches Christians have applied to their particular cultural environment, traces cross-cultural exchanges in contextual theology, and identifies themes in conversations on liturgical inculturation. In this true model of interdisciplinary work, Witvliet pulls a diverse array of voices together to examine questions surrounding cultural forces and liturgical practices.

Index

40, 48, 51, 52, 53, 54, 63, 64, 65, 66, 68, 69, 70, 71, 72, 74, 75, 83, 87, 92, 94–103, 104, 107, 108, 109, 111, 117, 121, 126, 132

Ordinance, 13, 17, 37, 47, 56, 104–7

Pentecostalism, 10, 25, 74, 75, 88

Perón, Juan, 3–4, 10, 30–31, 51, 63, 77

Plymouth Brethren, 4, 16, 18, 20, 28, 29, 32–34, 48, 51, 60, 74, 75

Prayer, 15, 18, 19, 27, 31–38, 51, 52, 53, 54, 55, 57, 58, 59, 61, 62, 63, 65, 66, 68, 70, 71, 72, 73, 76, 77, 78, 79, 82, 83, 86, 87, 88, 90, 92, 105, 109, 111, 118, 125

Preaching, 5, 15, 17, 18, 20, 27, 29, 31–34, 36, 38, 60, 61, 63, 64, 65, 70, 73, 74, 75, 87, 90, 92, 100, 104–9, 118, 127, 135

Roman Catholicism, conflicts with, 3–5, 10, 16,

17–20, 25, 27, 30–31, 33–34, 37, 50, 51, 52, 55, 56, 58, 63, 66, 73–74, 79–81, 84, 88, 91–93, 104–7, 110, 124

Rosas, Juan Manuel de, 3

Sacrament. *See* Ordinance

Scripture, 3, 4, 5, 11, 13, 17, 18, 19, 20, 25–26, 27, 29, 31, 32, 34–37, 38, 52, 53, 54, 55, 56, 58, 60, 61, 63, 64, 65, 71, 73, 74, 77, 78, 79, 80, 81, 82, 83, 84, 85, 86, 90, 92, 93, 106, 111, 112, 116, 118, 121, 126, 130, 135

Sermon. *See* Preaching

Sunday school, 28, 54, 62, 63, 68, 72, 84–85, 117, 128

Testimony, 15, 17, 18, 20, 34, 38, 51, 52–54, 56, 62, 63, 66, 68, 70, 71, 68, 86, 87, 90, 103, 118, 130

Tract, 5, 17, 29, 38, 44, 52, 53, 54, 55, 60, 62, 79, 85, 90